T0268656

ZERO AT THE BONE

ZERO
AT THE BONE

Fifty Entries Against Despair

CHRISTIAN
WIMAN

FARRAR, STRAUS AND GIROUX
NEW YORK

Farrar, Straus and Giroux
120 Broadway, New York 10271

Owing to limitations of space, all acknowledgments
for permission to reprint previously published material
can be found on pages 301–306.

Library of Congress Cataloging-in-Publication Data
Names: Wiman, Christian, 1966– author.
Title: Zero at the bone : fifty entries against despair / Christian Wiman.
Description: First edition. | New York : Farrar, Straus and Giroux, 2023.
Identifiers: LCCN 2023026123 | ISBN 9780374603458 (hardcover)
Subjects: LCGFT: Essays. | Poetry. | Creative nonfiction. |
    Literary criticism.
Classification: LCC PS3573.I47843 Z34 2023 | DDC 818/.54—
    dc23/eng/20230626
LC record available at https://lccn.loc.gov/2023026123

Designed by Gretchen Achilles

Our books may be purchased in bulk for promotional,
educational, or business use. Please contact your local bookseller
or the Macmillan Corporate and Premium Sales Department
at 1-800-221-7945, extension 5442, or by email
at MacmillanSpecialMarkets@macmillan.com.

www.fsgbooks.com
www.twitter.com/fsgbooks • www.facebook.com/fsgbooks

5   7   9   10   8   6

For Danielle, Eliza, and Fiona
a whole new naivete

But in good truth I've wandered much of late,
And sometimes, to my shame I speak, have need
Of my best prayers to bring me back again.

— WILLIAM WORDSWORTH,
"The Ruined Cottage"

CONTENTS

ZERO AT THE BONE

ZERO

To write a book against despair implies an intimate acquaintance with the condition. Otherwise what would be the point?

To write an introduction implies something to introduce, and I have no idea what this book will be. This is salvo, self-challenge, zero at the bone.

Well, one idea. I have published poetry, translation, criticism, theology, memoir, anthologies. They come out discretely, but I don't experience them that way. When I'm working, I lurch from one thing to another, I read twenty books at a time, I flit and havoc and half drown. I want to write a book true to the storm of forms and needs, the intuitions and impossibilities, that I feel myself to be. That I feel life to be.

When you're young, if you're at all "artistic," despair has an alluring quality. You affect it, deploy it, stroke it gently like a sedated leopard. Eventually the drug wears off. The drug of youth, I mean. There never was a leopard. It's just you, time piled up like volcanic detritus around you, miles and miles of silence. Who are you now? Which way is home? And what, pray tell, is the source of this slowly rousing growl?

I WILL LOVE YOU IN THE SUMMERTIME

Thirty years ago, watching some television report about depression and religion—I forget the relationship but apparently there was one—a friend who was entirely secular asked me with genuine curiosity and concern: "Why do they believe in something that doesn't make them happy?" I was an ambivalent atheist at that point, beset with an inchoate loneliness and endless anxieties, contemptuous of Christianity but addicted to its aspirations and art. I was also chained fast to the rock of poetry, having my liver pecked out by the bird of a harrowing and apparently absurd ambition— and thus had some sense of what to say. One doesn't follow God in hope of happiness but because one senses—miserable flimsy little word for that beak in your bowels—a truth that renders ordinary contentment irrelevant. There are some hungers that only an endless commitment to emptiness can feed, and the only true antidote to the plague of modern despair is an absolute—and perhaps even annihilating—awe. "I prayed for wonders instead of happiness," writes the great Jewish theologian Abraham Joshua Heschel, "and You gave them to me."

———

I thought of this moment not long ago when one of my twin four-year-old daughters walked wide-eyed and trembly into my room at midnight. My wife was traveling. The girls are accustomed to me being gone and have learned to allay their anxieties with the prospect of airport presents, but they are less sanguine about the absence of their mother. Still, I thought we were managing pretty well. There had been a vociferous territorial dispute at the kiddie pool, and then a principled aesthetic disagreement (over the length of my hair in a chalk drawing) was decided by a bite. But dinner was lively, the ice-cream bribery effective, and after story-time, poem-time, I-love-you-time, I slipped out of their room without a fuss. About an hour later, though, I looked up to find my blond-haired blue-eyed scarily intelligent sprite of a child Eliza standing in the doorway.

"Daddy," she said, "I can't sleep. Every time I close my eyes I'm seeing terrible things."

I'm a lifelong insomniac. I used to freak my own parents out when I was a small child by creeping quietly into their room and opening up their eyelids with my fingers in an effort—so the story goes—to see what they were dreaming, and in fact I began this very essay between two and four one morning when "my thoughts were all a case of knives," to quote the great seventeenth-century poet and priest George Herbert. So I was sympathetic to my daughter's plight.

I suggested she pray to God. This was a moment of either great grace or brazen hypocrisy (not that the two can't coincide), as I'm not a great pray-er myself and tend to be either undermined by irony or overwhelmed by my own chaotic consciousness. Nevertheless, I suggested that my little girl get down on her knees and bow her head and ask God to give her good thoughts, like the old family house in Tennessee that we'd gone to just a couple of weeks earlier, for example, the huge green yard with its warlock willows and mystery thickets, the river with its primordial snapping turtles and water-bearded cattle, the buckets of just-picked blueberries and the fried Krispy Kremes and the fireflies smearing their alien radiance through the humid Tennessee twilight. I told her to hold that image in her head and ask God to preserve it for her. I suggested she let the force of her longing and the fact of God's love coalesce into a form as intact and atomic as matter itself, to attend to memory with the painstaking attentiveness of the poet, the abraded patience of the saint, the visionary innocence of the child whose unwilled wonder erases any distinction between her days and her dreams. I said all this—underneath my actual words, as it were—and waited while all that blond-haired blue-eyed intelligence took it in.

"Oh, I don't think so Daddy." She looked me right in the eyes.

"What do you mean, Eliza, why not?"

"Because in Tennessee I asked God to turn me into a unicorn and"—she spread her arms wide in a disconcertingly adult and ironic shrug—"look how that's worked out."

———

What exactly does that mean: *to pray*? And is it something one ought to be teaching a child to do? And if we assume for a moment that it is indeed an essential thing to "learn," then what exactly ought one to pray for? A parking space? To be cured of some dread disease? For the emotional and spiritual well-being of a beloved child? To be a unicorn? For one night of untroubled sleep?

The Polish poet Anna Kamieńska died in 1986, at the age of sixty-six. She had converted to Christianity decades earlier, in her thirties, after the unexpected death of her beloved husband, the poet Jan Śpiewak. People who have been away from God tend to come back by one of two ways: extreme lack or extreme love, an overmastering sorrow or a strangely disabling joy. Either the world

7

is not enough for the hole that has opened in you, or it is too much. The two impulses are intimately related and it may be that the most authentic spiritual existence inheres in being able to perceive one state when you are squarely in the midst of the other. The mortal sorrow that shadows even the most intense joy. The immortal joy that can give even the darkest sorrow a fugitive gleam.

Anna Kamieńska, then. A devoted and tormented Catholic, her faith brought her great comfort and great anguish, often at the same time. No doubt this is precisely the quality that attracted me to her when I first came across a couple of passages from her diaries, high in the air above downtown Chicago in Northwestern Memorial Hospital, blood in my tubes and blades in my veins. I had—have—cancer. I have been living with it—dying with it— for so long now that it bores me, or baffles me, or drives me into the furthest crannies of literature and theology in search of something that will both speak and spare my own pain. Were it not for my daughters I think by this point I would be at peace with any outcome, which is, I have come to believe, one reason—the least reason, but still—why they are here.

Not long before her death, Anna Kamieńska wrote what I think is her best poem (available in English, at any rate), a stark, haunting, and insidiously hopeful little gem called "A Prayer That Will Be Answered." The title is worth some stress, in both senses of that word: "A Prayer That *Will Be Answered*."

Lord let me suffer much
and then die

Let me walk through silence
and leave nothing behind not even fear

Make the world continue
let the ocean kiss the sand just as before

Let the grass stay green
so that the frogs can hide in it

so that someone can bury his face in it
and sob out his love

Make the day rise brightly
as if there were no more pain

And let my poem stand clear as a windowpane
bumped by a bumblebee's head

tr. by Clare Cavanagh and Stanisław Barańczak

This is an uncanny poem. It gives God all power (the continuance of the world) and no power (it was going to continue anyway). It is implicitly apophatic, you might say. That is, it erases what it asserts: it is a prayer to be reconciled to a world in which prayer *does not work*. "Ah my dear God! though I am clean forgot, / Let me not love thee, if I love thee not," wrote George Herbert at the end of one of his own greatest poems ("Affliction (I)"). "We pray God to be free of God," says the thirteenth-century mystic Meister Eckhart. Behind Kamieńska's poem, infusing it with an ancient and awful power, is the most wonderful and terrible prayer one can pray: "Not my will, Lord, but yours." That's Jesus in the Garden of Gethsemane before the Roman soldiers come to take him to his death, just after he has sweated blood, begged God to let the cup of suffering pass him by, and wept to leave this world that he has come to love so completely and, it seems, helplessly. And then: Not my will, Lord, but yours. It's difficult enough to pray a prayer like this when you're thinking of making some big life decision. It's damn near impossible when your actual life is on the line, or the life of someone you love, when all you want to pray is *help, help, help*.

Not my will, Lord, but yours.

Kamieńska's poem is uncanny in another way, too—and triumphant. "If you want me again," writes Walt Whitman near the end of "Song of Myself," "look for me under your boot-soles," and this poem has a similar ghosting effect, gives its author a kind of posthumous presence. "Let my poem stand clear as a windowpane / bumped by a bumblebee's head." This, it turns out, has happened. The poem is indeed as clear as a windowpane, and we the readers, all these decades after Kamieńska's death, are bumping our heads upon it. The prayer has been answered, and to feel the full effect of this poem is to feel a little ripple of spirit going right through the stark indifferent reality to which the poet sought to be reconciled.

———

For a long time I tried to write a poem that had as its first line "Are you only my childhood?" By "childhood" I meant not only the encompassing bubble of Baptist religiosity in which I was raised, but also that universally animate energy, that primal permeability of mind and matter that children both intuit and inhabit ("The park lives outside," as one of my little girls said to the other when they were going to sleep), that clear and endlessly creative existence that a word like "faith" can only stain. By "you" I meant "You." I took dozens of different tacks for the poem, but it was all will, and thus all wasted. Years passed. Then recently, in a half-dreaming state in the middle of the night, I heard myself ask the question again: "Are you only my childhood?" And from deep within the dream a voice—it was me, but the voice was not mine—said, with what seemed to be genuine interest and puzzlement: "Why do you say *only*?"

———

Ah my dear angry Lord,
Since thou dost love, yet strike;
Cast down, yet help afford;
Sure I will do the like.

I will complain, yet praise;
I will bewail, approve:
And all my sour-sweet days
I will lament, and love.

George Herbert again. It's likely he wrote the poem—"Bitter-Sweet," it's called—between the ages of thirty-seven and forty, when he had just swerved from a disappointing political career into parish ministry, was newly and very happily married, and obviously dying of tuberculosis. "All my sour-sweet days / I will lament, and love." Destitution and abundance. Submission to God and aggression against God. What might it mean to pray an honest prayer? Maybe it means, like Meister Eckhart, praying to be free of the need for prayer. Maybe it means praying to be fit for, worthy of, capable of living up to, the only reality that we know, which is this physical world around us, the severest of whose terms is death.

Maybe it means resisting this constriction with the little ripple of spirit that cries otherwise, as all art, even the most apparently despairing, ultimately does. And maybe, just maybe, it even means praying for a parking spot in the faith that there is no permutation of reality too minute or trivial for God to be altogether absent from it. If Jesus's first miracle can be a kind of pointless party trick—he turns water into wine! Voilà!—maybe the lesson we are meant to learn from this is that we have to turn *everything* over to God, including those niggling feelings and hesitations we have that the whole rigmarole of sifting scripture like bird's entrails, and bowing one's suddenly brainless head, and "believing" in something more than matter—this is all just a little ridiculous, isn't it? An embarrassment even. The province, perhaps, of little children.

————

I can't tell a story of one daughter without including the other. Fiona, then. The olive-skinned and night-eyed child, the lithe and little trickster sister: Fiona.

When our girls were just two years old we spent a summer in Seattle, where I'd lived many years earlier. It was the first break I'd managed to take from my editing job in a decade, and it was only eight months after I'd undergone a bone marrow transplant. Time had a texture that summer, an hourly reality that we could taste and see. The girls went to a wonderful little day care in the mornings so my wife and I could write, and then we all came together in the afternoons to do something fun in the city. We adhered to the same nightly ritual that we did at home. I read to the girls and tucked them in before my wife took over, and the last thing I said every night was "I love you," to which they always replied promptly, "I love you, too, Daddy."

But then one night after my declaration Fiona was silent. She just kept staring at the ceiling.

"Do you love me, too, Fiona?" I asked, foolishly.

A long moment passed.

"No, Daddy, I don't."

"Oh, Fiona sweetie, I bet you do," I said.

Nothing.

"Well," I said finally, "I love you, Finn, and I'll see you in the morning."

And then as I started to get up, I felt her small hand on my arm and she said dreamily, without looking at me, like a little Lauren Bacall, "I will love you in the summertime, Daddy. I will love you . . . in the summertime."

I've told this to a couple of people who thought it was heartbreaking, but I was so proud I thought my heart would burst. *I will love you in the summertime.* What a piercing poetic thing to say—at two years old. And for weeks I thought about it. A year later, just after that dream I relate above, I even wrote a poem about it. *I will love you in the summertime.* Which is to say, given the charmed life we were living there in Seattle and all the grace and grief that my wife and I felt ourselves moving through at every second: I will love you in the time where there is time for everything, which is now and always. I will love you in the time when time is no more.

Now, do I think that's what my Athena-eyed and mysteriously interior two-year-old daughter meant by that expression? No, I do not. But do I think that sometimes life and language break each other open to change, that a rupture in one can be a rapture in the other, that sometimes there are, as it were, words underneath the words—even the very Word underneath the words? Yes, I do.

———

When Jesus says that you must become as little children in order to enter the kingdom of heaven, he is not suggesting that you must shuck all knowledge and revert to an innocence—or, worse, a state of helpless dependence—that you have lost or outgrown. The operative word in the injunction is "become." (The Greek word is *strepho*, which is probably more accurately translated as "convert," a word that more explicitly suggests an element of will and maturation.) Spiritual innocence is not beyond knowledge but inclusive of it, just as it is of joy and love, despair and doubt. For the hardiest souls, even outright atheism may be an essential element. ("There are two atheisms of which one is a purification of the notion of God," says Simone Weil.) There is some way of ensuring that one's primary intuitions survive one's secondary self; or, to phrase it differently, ensuring that one's *soul* survives one's self; or, to phrase it differently, to ensure that one's self and one's soul are not terminally separate entities. To *ripen* into childhood, as Bruno Schulz puts it.

So perhaps one doesn't teach children about God so much as help them grow into what they already know, and perhaps "know" is precisely the wrong verb. "Trying to solve the problem of God is like trying to see your own eyeballs," wrote Thomas Merton. It has been my experience that most adults will either smile wryly at this and immediately agree, or roll their eyes and lament the existence of this benighted superstition that pretzels intelligence into these pointless knots, this zombie zeal that will not die. It has also been my experience that there are on this earth two little children who, if told this koan by a father inclined to linguistic experiments, will separately walk over to the mirror and declare that in fact, Daddy, they *can* see their own eyeballs.

"I want only with my whole self to reach the heart of obvious truths." Thus Anna Kamieńska near the end of the fractured, intense, diamond-like diaries that circle around and around the same obsessive concern: God. I know just what she means. The trouble, though, as her own life and mind illustrate, is that, just as there are simple and elegant equations that emerge only at the end of what seems like a maze of complicated mathematics, so there are truths that depend upon the very contortions they untangle. Every person has to *earn* the clarity of common sense, and every path to that one clearing is difficult, circuitous, and utterly, painfully individual.

Here's an obvious truth: I am somewhat ambivalent about religion—and not simply the institutional manifestations, which even a saint could hate, but sometimes, too many times, all of it, the very meat of it, the whole goddamned shebang. Here's another: I believe that the question of faith—which is ultimately separable from the question of "religion"—is the single most important question that any person asks in and of her life, and that every life is an answer to this question, whether she has addressed it consciously or not.

As for myself, I have found faith to be not a comfort but a provocation to a life I never seem to live up to, an eruption of joy that evaporates the instant I recognize it as such, an agony of absence that assaults me like a psychic wound. As for my children, I would like them to be free of whatever particular kink there is in me that turns every spiritual impulse into anguish. Failing that, I would like them to be free to make of their anguish a means of peace, for themselves or others (or both), with art or action (or both). Failing that—and I suppose, ultimately, here in the ceaseless machinery of implacable matter, there is only failure—I would like them to be able to pray, keeping in mind the fact that, as Saint Anthony of the Desert said, a true prayer is one that you do not understand.

———

Typically cryptic, God said three weasels
slipping electric over the rocks
one current conducting them up the tree
by the river in the woods of the country
into which I walked
away and away and away;
and a moon-blued, cloud-strewn night sky
like an X-ray
with here a mass and there a mass
and everywhere a mass;
and to the tune of a two-year-old
storm of atoms
elliptically, electrically alive—
I will love you in the summertime, Daddy.
I will love you . . . in the summertime.

Once in the west I lay down dying
to see something other than the dying stars
so singularly clear, so unassailably there,
they made me reach for something other.
I said I will not bow down again
to the numinous ruins.
I said I will not violate my silence with prayer.
I said *Lord, Lord*
in the speechless way of things
that bear years, and hard weather, and witness.

THE WORLD SOUNDS

This may be my favorite poem. In all of poetry, I mean. On some days, of crepuscular mood and need.

DOMINATION OF BLACK

At night, by the fire,
The colors of the bushes
And of the fallen leaves,
Repeating themselves,
Turned in the room,
Like the leaves themselves
Turning in the wind.
Yes: but the color of the heavy hemlocks
Came striding.
And I remembered the cry of the peacocks.

The colors of their tails
Were like the leaves themselves
Turning in the wind,
In the twilight wind.
They swept over the room,
Just as they flew from the boughs of the hemlocks
Down to the ground.

I heard them cry—the peacocks.
Was it a cry against the twilight
Or against the leaves themselves
Turning in the wind,
Turning as the flames
Turned in the fire,
Turning as the tails of the peacocks
Turned in the loud fire,
Loud as the hemlocks
Full of the cry of the peacocks?
Or was it a cry against the hemlocks?

Out of the window,
I saw how the planets gathered
Like the leaves themselves
Turning in the wind.
I saw how the night came,
Came striding like the color of the heavy hemlocks.
I felt afraid.
And I remembered the cry of the peacocks.

Wallace Stevens

I don't know what this poem means, except that it means more than I know. It teaches me nothing, unless the surge of spiritual alertness it sends through my nerves counts as an increment of knowledge.

"Spiritual"? What other word should one use for a poem about death that makes one feel so alive?

Death? Is that what the poem is about then? In one sense, obviously: the hemlocks, the fear that starts at home (one man's death) but by the end has become cosmic (the death of all human endeavor, I think, the Great No that nibbles at consciousness, that *is*, in some way, consciousness). It means everything, of course, that for the fallen leaves (elegiacally lovely, one assumes), and the crackling fire, and even the dramatic slashes of the peacock tails, there is that *domination of black*.

Or it means almost everything. Music is moral, says Settembrini in *The Magic Mountain*, insofar as it has the power to be both stimulant and narcotic, to wake one up to life and to put one to sleep. "Domination of Black" seems to me as close as poetry can come to pure music and still be poetry—or at least the sort of poetry that I enjoy, I should say, for there are certainly other poems, including some by Stevens, that more completely slip free from the gravity of actual denotation. Such escape is not possible here, because this poem is conscious. It wakes one up. Thus, moral.

But Settembrini's dichotomy, like all dichotomies, is reductive. The poem both lulls and prods, wakes and sedates. It has the force of a spell or charm.

Wakes one up to what? "The danger," writes Simone Weil, "is not lest the soul should doubt whether there is any bread, but lest, by a lie, it should persuade itself that it is not hungry." Poetry attests to this abiding hunger, even when, perhaps especially when, the poet has lost all sense of the source and does nothing but cry out. "At a time like the present," Weil continues, "incredulity may be equivalent to the dark night of Saint John of the Cross if the unbeliever loves God, if he is like the child who does not know whether there is bread anywhere, but who cries out because he is hungry."

Or, in another key: "Unreal things have a reality of their own, in poetry as elsewhere" (Stevens).

———

"Unreal." A slippery word. It can mean false, used to dismiss a movie with plot holes or a sentimental novel. On the other hand, it can mean truer than we knew was possible: *Unreal*, the tourist says staring down into the Grand Canyon. In the first instance, we are frustrated and balked. An experience has been denied us, even as it has reminded us that we have had such experiences in the past. In the second, we are seized and enlarged. We are also— insofar as any experience of awe comes with a charge to act upon it, and insofar as an increased capacity for contemplation constitutes action—called.

But Stevens is using the word in a third sense, which in a way fuses the first two. He is referring to the forms that the imagination both perceives and creates. (Any work of true imagination, I would argue, always fuses those two actions.) There is inevitably an element of falseness to these forms, a factitiousness, as Plato suggested. And there is, though not inevitably, a sharp eruption of truth (or, if that word makes you nervous, a sense of enlarged or clarified or salvaged reality), as any experience of genuine art reveals.

Unreal things have a reality of their own. They will exert their force upon you whether or not you recognize them, but only when they are recognized can they become part of the reality that we usually refer to when we say that word. You have to assent to the invisible if you are ever to see it.

Seeing the Invisible is in fact the title of a monograph by the French philosopher Michel Henry on the work of Wassily Kandinsky. Henry believed that abstract art in general, and Kandinsky in particular, was not simply a development in the history of art, but the formal fruition of the hunger to truly see—and thereby to truly *be*—that has animated every work ever made. Artists were never in pursuit of the physical world per se. They were in pursuit of the force that forced them to pursue. "Life," Henry calls it. It's as good a word as any.

Art, if one really reflects on it and makes an exception of the Greeks, has only rarely been concerned with external reality. The world becomes the aim of an activity that ceases to be creative and lapses into representation and imitation only after its initial theme and true interest has been lost. The initial theme of art and its true interest is life. At its outset, all art is sacred, and its sole concern is the super-natural. This means that it is concerned with life—not with the visible but the invisible. Why is life sacred? Because we experience it within ourselves as something we have nei-ther posited nor willed, as something that passes through us without ourselves as its cause—we can only be and do anything whatsoever because we are carried by it. This pas-sivity of life to itself is our pathetic subjectivity—this is the invisible, abstract content of eternal art and painting.

According to Nina Kandinsky, her husband would create spe-cial colors for some paintings, colors that had never before existed, which he would then throw away once the painting was com-pleted so that the color could never be replicated. He didn't do this to create something original *to him*. He did it to honor, to participate in, the eternally dynamic nature of reality. "The world sounds," Kandinsky wrote. "It is a cosmos of spiritually affective be-ings. Thus, dead matter is living spirit." The most obvious way of reading this thought is that matter is pregnant with spirit. Reality is always in excess of perception, and any work (or life) that does not acknowledge this excess (and this splendid ignorance) is not only missing much of reality, but is itself *unreal* in the worst sense.

But there's another implication, which is not necessarily mutually exclusive. Kandinsky's image could suggest a sort of claustrophobic finitude: Instead of spirit animating and brimming from matter, what if, sometimes, it is trapped within it? Many writers have written about the liberating experience of great art, but what if we are not the only ones being freed? "The feeling remains," wrote Teresa of Ávila, "that God is on the journey too."

SO TRUED TO A ROAR

So trued to a roar,
so accustomed to a grimace
of against, I hardly noticed
it was over.

Like an invalid I crept
out into the open
(since when was there an open?)
and like a revenant lipped

the names of things
turned things again:
white pine, quaking aspen,
shagbark that by all rights

should have been shorn.
Was it for this, I asked
(since when was there someone to ask?)
that I was born?

No answer, unless of leaves
acquiring light, and small lives
going about their business
of being less,

and on the clear pond
(and in the clearer beyond)
the mien of a man
unraptured back to man.

A STRONGER NAME FOR LIFE

"Abstract" no longer refers to what is derived from the world at the end of a process of simplification or complication or at the end of the history of modern painting; instead, it refers to what was prior to the world and does not need the world in order to exist.

Michel Henry, *Seeing the Invisible: On Kandinsky*

The belief that words in themselves have the power to make things happen—especially words in extraordinary combinations—is one of the distinguishing features of native American thought; and it may be said that for the people who share this belief a connection exists between the sacred and the verbal, or, to put it in more familiar terms, a connection between religion and poetry . . . Not surprisingly, the word "poetry," as it is understood in English today, has no precise equivalent in native American languages. What are thought of by outsiders as Indian "poems" are actually spells, prayers, or words to songs. Though often appreciated as beautiful, they are seldom recited purely for entertainment. Rather, they are used for gaining control or for making things turn out right.

John Bierhorst, *The Sacred Path: Spells, Prayers & Power Songs of the American Indians*

In the realm of primal words, we are always on the verge of tautology.

Josef Pieper, *Happiness and Contemplation*

The relative is absolute, and judgment
Genius, and the point of stasis, where
You say it is. O mind beyond compare,
In what doubt, or in what impersonal
Intention, even tentative and small,
Shall you perceive an other than your will?

Edgar Bowers, "The Philosophical Life"

One cannot speak of God simply by speaking of man in a loud voice.

Karl Barth, *The Word of God and the Word of Man*

. . . for you know as well as I do that under certain circumstances, at a certain temperature, metaphorically speaking, words lose their substance, their content, their meaning, they simply deliquesce, so that in this vaporous state deeds alone, naked deeds, show any tendency to solidity, it is deeds alone that we can take in our hands, so to speak, and examine like a mute lump of mineral, like a crystal.

Imre Kertész, *Kaddish for an Unborn Child*

Here it is enough to mention that Merleau-Ponty's view of language as a thoroughly incarnate medium, of speech as rhythm and expressive gesture, and hence of spoken words and phrases as active sensuous presences afoot in the material landscape (rather than as ideal forms that represent, but are not a part of, the sensuous world)—goes a long way toward helping us understand the primacy of language and word magic in native rituals of transformation, metamorphosis, and healing. *Only if words are felt, bodily presences, like echoes or waterfalls, can we understand the power of spoken language to influence, alter, and transform the perceptual world.* As this is expressed in a Modoc song:

I
the song
I walk here

David Abram, *The Spell of the Sensuous*

Foolishly, she had set them opposite each other. That could be remedied tomorrow. If it were fine, they should go for a picnic. Everything seemed possible. Everything seemed right. Just now (but this cannot last, she thought, dissociating herself from the moment while they were all talking about boots) just now she had reached security; she hovered like a hawk suspended; like a flag floated in an element of joy which filled every nerve of her body fully and sweetly, not noisily, solemnly rather, for it arose, she thought, looking at them all eating there, from husband and children and friends; all of which rising in this profound stillness (she was helping William Bankes to one very small piece more, and peered into the depths of the earthenware pot) seemed now for no special reason to stay there like a smoke, like a fume rising upwards, holding them safe together. Nothing need be said; nothing could be said. There it was, all round them. It partook, she felt, carefully helping Mr. Bankes to a specially tender piece, of eternity; as she had already felt about something different once before that afternoon; there is a coherence in things, a stability; something, she meant, is immune from change, and shines out (she glanced at the window with its ripple of reflected lights) in the face of the flowing, the fleeting, the spectral, like a ruby; so that again tonight she had the feeling she had had once today, already, of peace, of rest. Of such moments, she thought, the thing is made that endures.

Virginia Woolf, *To the Lighthouse*

I think we must be faithful to immortality, that other, slightly stronger name for life.

Boris Pasternak, *Doctor Zhivago*

CAN THIS SIN LIVE

To be conscious is to be conscious of suffering. Our own pain wakes us to the pain of others. These are truisms, which like most truisms gloss a complicated truth. Pain erases other people as often as it engenders sympathy for them. We may become more conscious, but consciousness itself becomes a cage. This imprisonment can take many forms: an idolatry of suffering as a form of knowledge or spiritual good, an outrage that no person (or group) has suffered as we have, or simply a solipsistic withdrawal that leaves us maniacally describing every detail of our cells. And selves. We are our wounds, it seems, and without them will not exist. It's a hard paradox, though, that to understand the truth of one's particular experience of suffering may mean sacrificing that very particularity.

BOUQUET

i have gathered my losses
into a spray of pain;
my parents, my brother,
my husband, my innocence
all clustered together
durable as daisies.
now i add you,
little love, little

flower,
who walked unannounced
into my life
and almost blossomed there.

The loss in this poem by Lucille Clifton could be anything. It could be a miscarriage, a friendship, a romantic relationship that flared and failed. It could be a dog. A biographer will no doubt land decisively on a subject one day—and will thereby fall short of this small poem's real scope and accomplishment. Even if Clifton had a certain loss in mind, the poem, as true poems will, has leapt beyond one woman's existence into existence itself. One thinks of one's own life and all the almost-loves that failed—often because one failed them—to blossom.

One grows so tired, in American public life, of the certitudes and platitudes, the megaphone mouths and stadium praise, influencers and effluencers and the whole tsunami of slop that comes pouring into our lives like toxic sludge. One wants a teller in a time like this.

MISS ROSIE

when i watch you
wrapped up like garbage
sitting, surrounded by the smell
of too old potato peels
or
when i watch you
in your old man's shoes

with the little toe cut out
sitting, waiting for your mind
like next week's grocery
i say
when i watch you
you wet brown bag of a woman
who used to be the best looking gal in georgia
used to be called the Georgia Rose
i stand up
through your destruction
i stand up

In a video online Clifton rejects—*firmly*—one apparently obvious reading of this poem, in which the poet's vision of the woman is negative, or at least ambivalent. But poems have a life apart from the poet's own. In this reading, the violence the woman has suffered intensifies the vision the poet is granted. The detached appraisal—"wrapped up like garbage," "waiting for your mind"—is bound up with survival. An awful thing to posit. But the reading is there; the poem has leapt beyond the poet's intentions. "When I watch you," Clifton says three times in this short poem, as if the act of attention were as important as its object, "i stand up / through your destruction." "Through" meaning both "in spite of" (and in solidarity with) and "by means of" (separate from). As I say, an awful thing to posit. Turn the poem one way and you hear it as a whisper. Turn it again and you hear brazen defiance. The trick is to hold the poem at just the angle where neither reading predominates.

The smallness of Clifton's poems does make, in total, a large statement. Which is: I have been almost crushed by this culture's gargantuanism and idolatry of power. I will not play your game (even the rigorous lowercase contributes to this*). I will not swagger. I will not pretend to know more than I do. Or less.

SLAVESHIPS

loaded like spoons
into the belly of Jesus
where we lay for weeks for months
in the sweat and stink
of our own breathing
Jesus
why do you not protect us
chained to the heart of the Angel
where the prayers we never tell
and hot and red
as our bloody ankles
Jesus
Angel
can these be men
who vomit us out from ships
called Jesus   Angel   Grace Of God
onto a heathen country
Jesus
Angel

---

* So different, for instance, from that of Cummings. Cummings's "I" is always calling attention to itself and the hyperactive style around it. Clifton's "I" is hardly recessive or meek. If anything, it's sharper for the way it fuses autonomy and anonymity—less assertion than incision.

ever again
can this tongue speak
can these bones walk
Grace Of God
can this sin live

Some slave ships really did bear the names *Jesus, Angel, Grace Of God*. Some places of worship on the west coast of Africa were located directly above holding cells for slaves awaiting transport. While men in fresh linen bowed their heads and thanked God for his bounty, that "bounty" sat in shackles and shit below, re-hearsing sufferings that would only grow immeasurably worse. How does one take seriously the love of God when it has been so thoroughly—and so often—transformed into an engine of death?

I met Lucille Clifton once. In 2007 she won the Ruth Lilly Poetry Prize for lifetime achievement, which I administered for a number of years as editor of *Poetry* magazine. It was, for a while, a perfect evening. Clifton came to the ceremony surrounded by extended family and exuded the kind of grounded and candid delight that is easy to share. ("That's my grandma!" a little girl cried out of the large audience when her grandma took the stage, to which Clifton said, "Now that's the best introduction one could ever get.") Then she read—sitting down, as I remember, for she was not in good health—all the poems I'm quoting here, with just the right balance of pride, gratitude, and acid.

Afterward, an exclusive group repaired to an exclusive restaurant in downtown Chicago. You know the place, aggressively velvet, waiters with the faces of fruit bats, a kind of blood pudding of "privilege." Sometimes I can't believe how long it has taken me to recognize, and thereby avoid, my revulsions. We had a private room with multiple tables. We must have spent hours there, must have tasted exquisite dishes and shared hilarities of poetry and life. I don't recall. It all dissolved in a single instant at the end, when a tall and leonine longtime board member, who had spent the entire evening locked in loud hate with his wife—drunk with years of drinking, drunk in that way that is no longer fleeing despair but deeply, fatally committed to it—lurched toward where we sat. *LouISE*, he bellowed above us, a kind of wrathful bonhomie about him, the golden boy gone old. *Wonderful. Just WONderful. LouISE.*

Can this sin live?

It's a cunningly subtle line, emblematic of much of Clifton's work. She is, of course, tweaking Ezekiel:

> And he said unto me, Son of man, can these bones live? And I answered, O Lord God, thou knowest.
> Again he said unto me, Prophesy upon these bones, and say unto them, O ye dry bones, hear the word of the Lord.
> Thus saith the Lord God unto these bones; Behold, I will cause breath to enter into you, and ye shall live.

> Ezekiel 37:3-5

This is a promise of resurrection, both of individuals and of a nation. The prophecy links divine power to human speech, the Word to the word, eternity to time, and amounts to an assurance that the life of God and the life of humans are so raveled together that neither, for either, will ever be completely lost. Clifton ironizes this reading, because one's immediate answer to the question of whether this *sin* can live is: Good God, let's hope not. Let's hope this whole sad chapter of human barbarism and religious perversion can mercifully and entirely die.

34

But the line slips free from that one reading. To invoke prophetic power is also, in this instance, to harness it. Something of the rhetorical force of that passage from Ezekiel, its clipped mystery and inspired wrath, survives in the lines of "slaveships." Also, inevitably, something of its hope. Ezekiel is writing after the fall of Jerusalem in 586 BC and the dispersal and enslavement of the Jewish people. Clifton is writing after sixty million Africans have been scattered and destroyed in the Atlantic slave trade. The Word comes streaming again through, *and by means of*, the word. In terms of the poem, Jesus (the man) is on board *Jesus* (the ship), but he is in the hold, just as, when the worship services took place above the captured slaves on the Gold Coast of Africa, God, if he was anywhere, was underneath it all, shackled and sweating and merged with human terror. "slaveships," then, is not only a question about the limits of sin, but also a question about the limits of grace. Is there a power capable of not simply casting the worst human evils into oblivion beyond further harm, but also a love that might actually transform them? Can this sin *live*?

"I have a capacity for love without / forgiveness," writes the contemporary African American poet Terrance Hayes, seeking to make sense of his relationship to Wallace Stevens, whose racism was at times explicit. Listen closely to Clifton's poems and you might begin to hear something similar, a capacity to make rage an embrace. It's a kind of prophetic intimacy she manages, a fusion of utterance and action. She includes you, no matter who you are.

WON'T YOU CELEBRATE WITH ME

won't you celebrate with me
what i have shaped into

a kind of life? i had no model.
born in babylon
both nonwhite and woman
what did i see to be except myself?
i made it up
here on this bridge between
starshine and clay,
my one hand holding tight
my other hand; come celebrate
with me that everyday
something has tried to kill me
and has failed.

[6]

ISSUES OF BLOOD

My wife and I learned something strange recently about our already strange dog, Mack, the midsize black-and-white mutt we've had for almost a decade. With his keg chest and stub legs, his hunter's nose and soulful eyes, he looks like a black Lab crammed into the body of a beagle. He was on doggy death row when we got him from a shelter in Alabama, and he was so odd and nervous that you could never tell what was going to turn his terrors on. More than once we returned home to find him paralyzed (for how long?) on a small rug or even a piece of newspaper as if he were stranded on an island amid dangers we couldn't see. Mack has been having some troubling health issues lately, and in the course of the vet's investigations there was an incidental finding: Mack has a bullet in him.

I can't overstate how disturbing this news was to us. It's not just the obvious disgust: to think of some miserable man—because of course it had to be a man—taking aim at this utterly docile and probably mentally impaired dog and blasting away. And then to think of Mack crawling off to die somewhere and then, somehow, not dying—for Mack is not only docile but, as our vet has told us, preternaturally tough. Dogs hide pain, they do not want you to be aware of it, but Mack will try to hide even his reaction to extreme procedures at the vet's office, as if he's learned that it does not pay, no matter what, to let a human know what you feel.

But it wasn't just the act itself that so disturbed us. No, what was really gut-wrenching, what left us both stunned and tearful in our

37

kitchen the day we talked to the vet on the phone, was thinking about Mack carrying around this memento of that violent moment for all these years. All the life that we had lived with Mack: the births of our daughters, my dire illnesses and miraculous recoveries, new cities and new careers. And to think of that sweet odd dog all the while dragging around that unspeakable—in both senses of the word—pain.

The Sunday after learning about Mack's bullet, I heard a sermon focused on the woman in Luke who suffers from an "issue of blood." The text says that she has suffered for twelve years and has spent all her money on doctors. Just imagine the contempt she would have endured at the hands of those men—again, they would have been men—her whole life defined by this one pain, which would have entailed shame and loneliness as well as physical suffering, since menstruating women were considered "unclean" and thus untouchable. So when she hears that there's this man, this Jesus, going around healing people, she thinks to herself, why not. Or no, that actually doesn't match the urgency in the passage at all. She doesn't think to herself "why not" but instead feels a compulsion in her heart that she does not understand but understands that it requires action. The scripture tells us that Jesus feels "virtue" or "power" go out of him, and maybe what this unnamed woman first felt when she heard the name of Jesus was pain going out of her—and she went to find the man who had the name that could make this miracle come to pass.

I've probably heard thirty sermons about this woman. The lesson is almost always about one's trust in God or lack thereof, the faith that can move mountains, bootstrap stuff. And indeed that was the gist of the sermon I heard a couple of weeks ago. I've always been intrigued by the story, but I've also felt a little remote from this woman with her "issue of blood," at least until I looked down last month and saw a whole different aspect to the dog with whom I have shared a life for the past ten years. John Keats once said that no tenet of philosophy is ever really accepted in us until it is proved on our pulses. Scripture is no different. I don't care how many passion plays you've wept at. Until someone you truly love slips out of this world forever, the pain and promise of Christ remain abstract. That's all right, so long as you let Christ's reality— which is to say, simply, *reality*—work against that abstraction in your heart.

Here's an example. The very week I learned about Mack's bullet, I was teaching the notebooks and letters of Etty Hillesum. "Etty"—as she always called herself—is twenty-seven years old in 1941 when, in German-occupied Amsterdam, she begins to keep a diary. The vise is tightening. Jews have to wear yellow stars and their rights are being steadily eroded. There are fewer and fewer opportunities for them to make a living, more and more places where they are not even allowed to walk, and people are beginning to disappear. Etty writes all this down along with her own sometimes serious and sometimes frivolous concerns, and then an odd thing begins to happen. She starts addressing God directly. This is odd because, though Jewish, Etty was raised in a thoroughly secular, intellectual house devoid of all religious "sentiment," as her father called it, and hitherto she has had no religious impulse or awareness at all. But God is becoming painfully and joyfully apparent to Etty Hillesum, as is the role to which he is calling her. "There must be someone to live through it all," she says, "and bear witness to the fact that God lived, even in these times." She determines that she will be "the thinking heart of the barracks."

And that is precisely what she becomes. Westerbork was a transit camp originally designed to house fifteen hundred Jews who had fled Germany before Germany invaded Holland. By the time

Etty went there—voluntarily, at first, as she could not bear being separated from her imprisoned family—there were some forty thousand Jews crammed into barracks so miserable that disease, despair, and suicide were endemic. Every Monday a train pulled into the station and loaded up the next list of people who had been chosen for Auschwitz. It was an anteroom of hell, and they all knew it. And yet Etty wrote that her months "behind razor wire," as she put it, when she spent her days attending to the suffering of others and to the unkillable beauty of the natural world, had turned out to be the happiest time of her life, and that she had in fact "learned to love Westerbork." This would be miracle enough, but it's not all. The truly striking thing about the late entries of these diaries, which end with a postcard thrown from the window of the train bearing her away to death ("We left the camp singing"), is that Etty refuses to hate.

Etty Hillesum was never a Christian (though she was deeply familiar with, and moved by, the Gospels), but she does seem to me to embody Christ's message in an exemplary way. And what is that message? That there is not a person reading these words, there is not a friend or family member from whom you feel utterly estranged, there is not even a solipsistic and apparently unsalvageable man sitting in the White House* who does not have, festering somewhere, a bullet in them. Sitting down to write these thoughts was the first time I have ever considered all the other people around Jesus when he healed that woman with the issue of blood. They, too, had their issues of blood. It's a wonder Jesus didn't shatter from the sheer pressure of all those *unspeakable* pains around him. But then, eventually, I guess he did.

Rowan Williams, echoing Keats, says that there are lives that

* I wrote this in 2017, though it doesn't matter in terms of the larger point.

speak to us as no precept ever can. They reveal to us a wondrous country of which they are natives, and they make us say: whatever peace that person has, I want and need. And it just so happens that the illuminated life that Williams is describing in this passage was lived by . . . Etty Hillesum. Few of us will ever be called to witness world pain—to Weltschmerz—as Etty was, but I feel sure that there is some one pain to which every one of us is called to witness and perhaps ease. It might be as simple as a phone call to a family member you haven't spoken to in too long, it might be some thorn in the heart of a friend to whom you have not paid sufficient attention, it might be some wholly ordinary encounter you have in the next few hours of this wholly ordinary day—when suddenly you feel some power going out of you. Christ may be in us. But ours are the only hands he has.

[7]

PARTICULAR FLESH

I. (SOME LUCK IS LOVE)

Thin as a filament and similarly inside
a sphere of purpose her burn enables,
she picks up her littlest
with one sharply modern arm,
one-hands from the third-hand van
a bag of apples for the evening's
crumble, and, as she calls out
to the unscared, floss-haired five-year-old
who's wandered toward the road,
wonders what it is,
among and within all that is,
that draws her feelings like filings
toward some single unsayable thing.

* * *

Midday, midforties, little Greta greeting leaves
as they helix down to the ground around her.
This is the time of happiness people look back on,
or try to, though like the etching that the acid stamps,
it takes pain to make a memory
and pain is precisely what is missing now.

Fall, Connecticut coming to consciousness,
the lengthening dark ablaze in all the trees.
Greta, ecstatic in that blast of lack.

* * *

This is still country enough for stars,
and sometimes, when the girls are asleep,
she and her husband keep faith with the fine madness
that first drew them to and through each other
to share a simple dinner in the dark backyard.
Grilled chicken, chilled lager, the monitor
with its green eye and innocuous squawks.
Strange to think of all of the stars that aren't,
of light as loss until it turns to time.

* * *

The door she's never thought to lock
is open when the neighbor needs some mayonnaise.
The Sunday they forgot to change the clock
they missed the preaching and went straight to praise.

Sometimes a season seems a gust of wind,
sometimes a lifetime gravitates to one noon's green.
Some griefs are keepsakes from a place you've never been.
Some luck is love incompletely seen.

* * *

Grabbing Greta, snipping basil,
reading Augustine on the elliptical

("Our whole reward is seeing"),
begetting and forgetting in one go,
her mind is like a skyline, lit with distance,
one life in which a million lives
strive, grieve, love, end, are.

I don't know who I was before Daniel happened. Didn't happen? I guess some would say that, have said it in their silences when I have once more given evidence of not "getting over" his death.

His death? *Born asleep,* his gravestone reads, which is at once right and so wrong that every time I stand there I feel going through me those same electric perceptions his sleep woke in me.

We were in the living room and Adam was talking about fixing the broken slats in the porch railing so the girls wouldn't fall and something in me just . . . stopped. No. Something in me wasn't in me but was—how to put it—with me. Grieving me, almost.

Here is what I mean. There is a time before and there is a time after, but there is no time. There is an entire life that didn't happen, which happens in me forever now.

Family gathered within a day, knit together by this death in a way that no new life would have done. Friends came from far away and filled our house with years we'd thought lost. A woman I know only from conversations in the nursery school parking lot, a woman raised so far outside of any church that God remains, I suppose, a dangerously volatile possibility in her, had a rapturous experience of sorrow during Daniel's memorial service. I don't want to think of grace growing out of such despair but part of what grace is, I am coming to realize, is being freed from wondering at its source.

Sometimes I lie in bed at night and feel another life beside mine. Not Daniel's. Mine. As if adjacency were my nature now. What do I mean? *This is not over*, the minister said, trying to comfort us. *We shall all be changed.*

Things like this don't happen to people like us. That's what my father said. We were standing on the back porch—Adam had already fixed it—and it was one of those blousy Autumn-almost-over days so temperate and noncommittal you don't notice until the first cold catches your attention and a whole slab of undifferentiated time moves through you like a ghost. One of those days when you are not quite you, standing there with your good father and the beautiful leaves and a sense that you must not move, must not even breathe wrong or a whole life is going to come tearing out of you like a scream. If things like that happened to people like you.

III. (FELLOWSHIP)

Tragedy and Christianity are incommensurable,
he declared, which we'd have chalked to bluster
had he not, within the month, held a son
hot from the womb but cold to his kiss,
and over a coffin compact as a toolbox wept
in the wrecked unreachable way that most resist,
and that all of us, where we are most ourselves,
turn away from.
              Bonded and islanded
by the silence, we waited there,
desperate, with our own pains, to believe,
desperate, with our own pains, not to.

IV. (GOD IS MY STRENGTH)

> The worst is not
> So long as we can say, "This is the worst."

Edgar in *King Lear*. A few lines earlier he has declared his suffering absolute, his decline and abasement complete. In between he has found his beloved father with his eyes gouged out, seeking a means of death. The whole play has often been read as an annihilation of hope, grief so great it precludes grief, forcing upon the characters (the ones left) and the audience (the ones conscious) a static and unredeemable despair. Strange, then, that it should be so often considered the pinnacle of English literature, as if the moral force of art were irrelevant, as if people lived as nihilistically as they read. Even stranger, perhaps, that one can walk out of a good production of *Lear*—which is *definitely* an expression of despair—both stricken and enlivened, numbed and newly alert; that staged pain should be, not simply a purge, as Aristotle said, but (to borrow the words of a later thinker) a provocation "to have life, and to have it more abundantly."

"The worst is not / So long as we can say, 'This is the worst.'" To speak extreme grief, as Rowan Williams has so eloquently expressed,* is to mark it as a thing that *can be spoken of*. It is to bring the abyss into the realm of consciousness; perhaps not into the realm of meaning, which would be to deform and falsely diminish it. But into the realm of time, which implies, if nothing else, the possibility of change.

A Pyrrhic consolation, to be sure. On the one hand, Edgar's speech implies that, no matter how dire our current circumstances,

---

* *The Tragic Imagination*

there awaits, if we can still breathe, some as yet inconceivable suffering ahead. On the other hand, his words suggest that even here, where life is so excruciating that our only surviving desire is to leave it, there is still a possibility for change. And where there is even a possibility for change, there is hope.

True hope goes backward as well as forward. It can transfigure a past we thought was petrified. It can give voice to certain silences or make us more fluent in silence itself. It can turn history into tragedy.

The story of Jesus is, in an inescapable sense, a tragedy. That God himself could be gone. That we could kill not simply what we most crave and love—"to have life, and to have it more abundantly"—but love itself. I am familiar with the doctrine of resurrection. I have read the apostle Paul: "If Christ has not been raised, our preaching is worthless, and so is our faith." I have even, on occasion, when faith and imagination have miraculously merged, managed to inhabit the elusive truth therein.

But resurrection *is* a function of faith and imagination. Suffering and death are facts. Resurrection we will never know, at least insofar as knowledge is bound to life and time. Suffering and death, at some point, will be *all* that we know.

"This is not over," the preacher cries, and he is right to do so, to remind the assembled of the holy and heroic absurdity of faith, of the knowing beyond knowledge. But one need not feel guilty not to feel it. Faith is a grace, not an achievement. And there are times in human existence when imagination as consolation is a violation of life and a desecration of grief. Here is what I mean:

The mind may sort it out and give it names—
When a man dies he dies trying to say without slurring
The abruptly decaying sounds. It is true

49

That only flesh dies, and spirit flowers without stop
For men, cows, dung, for all dead things; and it is good, yes—

But an incarnation is in particular flesh
And the dust that is swirled into a shape
And crumbles and is swirled again had but one shape
That was this man. When he is dead the grass
Heals what he suffered, but he remains dead,
And the few who loved him know this until they die.

Galway Kinnell, "Freedom, New Hampshire"

Almost exactly two years after his brother was born asleep, Gabriel was born awake. He is an entirely different existence. The tragedy is untouched. He is existence entirely different. The tragedy is touched with God.

Gabriel ("God is my strength") was the name of the angel who told Mary the miracle that was about to happen to, in, and *by means of* her. Are angels clairvoyant? The text is silent (though Mary, tellingly, is "troubled"). It's hard, though, not to see a shadow of sorrow flicker on that shining face.

I cried the first time I touched him, Gabriel, not with sorrow but with the shock of awe. The workings of his week-old fingers, the eon eyes, the smooth and placid brow to which nothing—to which everything—had happened.

8

THE MAN WHO PLANTED PEACE

Can't be done, they said,
what with the leeching weeks, the haywire sun.
And anyway why, given the blood, given the hunger,
given heaven.
(Or would have said, he knew, had he told them.)

Never mind the source. Never mind the seeds
numerous as the grass. Never mind the never
asserting itself like a migraine in matter.

Afterward, he lies between two furrows
until the warping earth, and the impastoed sky,
and his own intolerable heart, grow still.
Prayers—are they prayers?—
breeze through him like wind through a skull.

> *Cell, sap, bud*
> *Such wrung, such wrested things*
> *Flower, style, stigma*

They bloom at night, like four-o'clocks but later,
my midnights, he calls them, though it's usually two.
You have to get down on your knees to see:

minuscule, incandescently dark, each petal
intricately and perfectly curved, without origin or end.

And then each dawn: gone.
And not just withdrawn either,
but erased, expunged, unimaginable.
He stands alone in the field.

Two things are beyond him:
the moment they open and the moment they close.
Two truths are within him:
the moment they open —

> *and freedoms bound to now*
> *and silence synonymous with God*
> *and dawn a scald of joy*

— the moment they close.

You know where this is going.
One night nothing opens. And grows.
One night night is all there is.
And the man who planted peace,
who after all is only words,
disperses the minute your mind releases him,
and the moon is memory, and the stars are darkness,
and time itself seems to beat like a lullaby of bone.

9

THE KEEP

They made a place they made of pain
exacting the center of the misty city.
The moats are metaphorical,
the drawbridge always down.
All day every day at every hour
men and women, children, wheeled
into a world that is not the world,
but more so, to seam themselves to machines
from which the healing bane
drips. Screams are rare, but memorable,
mirrored in the faces of those
who do not make them. Through the rooms
the white minders come and go
with their upbeat and their bags of blood.
Their aspect is the aspect of souls
that, having seen the worst, work
forever now to see it through,
to see through it: a child on five
who's ceased to breathe; on ten
a collar bone like cooling lava.
They made a place, they made of pain,
because of what we know we build
the closest we can come to grace.

The moats are metaphorical,
which means exactly what we let it mean.
All day every day at every hour.
Their aspect is the aspect of souls.

10

A PRISON GETS TO BE A FRIEND

Hypothesis: there are creative writers, and there are destructive writers, and sometimes the destructive ones are a hell of a lot more creative, and sometimes both kinds emerge from one mind. (*The Waste Land* is destructive; its energy is against. *Four Quartets* is creative; it expresses and extends the existential unity that is its source.) By "creative" I mean disclosing and furthering reality, equipping human consciousness to grow. By "destructive" I mean waging an assault on the kinds of *un*consciousness that falsify, obscure, and deform reality. Again, the distinction is not necessarily qualitative, nor the categories cleanly distinct. And though most great writing falls in the former category, the latter is equally necessary. Human consciousness calcifies, our means of sensation and expression atrophy; sometimes we are well and truly petrified, and some radical detonation is required. Much of high modernism was such a blow. The trouble is when a writer whose gift is demolition is mistaken for one of the other, when a radioactive space is seen as a fine place to settle. Samuel Beckett, for instance. How many minor talents have wandered into the desert of his silences, and perished there.

———

Just because a work is creative doesn't mean it's pacific. It might be creating—that is, illuminating—a hellscape you have long avoided, and now need to make your way through.

A writer is not obligated to fight despair. Sometimes the best gift can be the starkest depiction of an intractable reality, that head-clearing unsquinting astringent allover intake of a truth.

> Sorrow was all my soul; I scarce believ'd,
> Till grief did tell me roundly, that I liv'd.

That's from what may be my favorite George Herbert poem, "Affliction (I)," which unlike most of his work ends without bringing the Good News: "Let me not love thee, if I love thee not."* The line is fine, though, between articulation and cultivation, between despair as affliction and despair as sustenance. One needn't be an artist to be prone to the latter, but modern art has really seasoned the feast.

———

Reading an intelligent, disaffected, much-celebrated young novelist so adept at ironizing his own existence, so masterful at noticing every detail of the (rarefied) collective consciousness within which he is enmeshed, that it seems crude to point to a first principle and say: there is your problem. Yet I keep thinking of Jürgen Moltmann writing about the cross: "It alienates alienated men, who have come to terms with alienation." I'm not saying that this novelist, who is Jewish, needs to turn to Jesus. I'm saying that he is not

---

* In other words: If my love is not real, please annihilate it. Or: If I can't love you properly, please let me go. Or, maybe most interestingly: If I can't love you properly, that is to say, if I can't love thee when thou art not, can't love the not-ness of you as much as I love your is-ness, then let the imperative to love God—let the very notion *of* God—be abolished in me.

disquieted enough by, seems in fact attached to, his own alienation. This is a toy despair. It's entertaining, brilliant at times, but it cannot help me.

———

From despair keep us, Aquin's dumb son;
From despair keep us, Saint Welcome One;
From lack of despair keep us, Djuna and John Donne.

Marie Ponsot, "Private and Profane"

———

By "against" in the subtitle of this book I don't mean to imply a "position." I'm not against despair in the way that I'm against, say, Donald Trump. In fact I'm sometimes very much in favor of despair when it's a realistic appraisal of odious circumstance—like Donald Trump. But despair, like most human qualities, can be both sinful and salvific. Acedia, for instance, is a kind of spiritual inertia, an uncontested torpor, and is in Catholicism a mortal sin. The dark night of the soul, on the other hand, is an annihilating but necessary prelude to a renewed awareness of God. At the moment, in truth, either would seem a relief to me. Would have a name and a pedigree. Fifty entries against despair? I think suddenly of the coffee I had with the poet whose fifth (and, as it turned out, final) book of poetry had just come out. I mentioned how different it seemed to me from her earlier work. "Yes," she said, "I wanted to destroy all that."

———

A Prison gets to be a friend—
Between its Ponderous face
And Ours—a Kinsmanship express—
And in its narrow Eyes—

We come to look with gratitude
For the appointed Beam
It deal us—stated as Our food—
And hungered for—the same—

Emily Dickinson, #652

———

"There's something obscene in a living person sitting by the fire and believing in God." The quote, from 1928, is familiar to anyone who loves Virginia Woolf. (She was referring to T. S. Eliot, who had just converted.) So is the dire end to which she came some thirteen years later when she loaded her coat pockets with heavy rocks, waded into the Ouse, and embraced the oblivion that she had spent a lifetime creating out of, and in spite of, and against. Again, as with the novelist above, something too crude in simply pointing to her quote and fate and saying: there's your problem, right there. Or is there? "You must become an ignorant man again / And see the sun with an ignorant eye." Another well-known quote, from another pagan saint: Wallace Stevens. Conversion, like creation, is ongoing. That's probably what Woolf, whose work is every bit as mystically provocative and transcendent as Eliot's, was reacting to after taking tea with the newly converted poet that day in London: the self-conscious (and, inevitably, self-ennobling) drama of it all, the notion that one could make a clean break with the furies of one's time and mind. That her words have a self-conscious (and self-ennobling) drama of their own—this only shows that her despair and Eliot's are facets of the same thing. A prison gets to be a friend.

———

My pilgrim's progress has been to climb down a thousand ladders until I could finally reach out a hand of friendship to the little clod of earth that I am.

Carl Jung, *Letters I: 1906–1950*

PROFESSOR OF THE PRACTICE OF RELIGION AND LITERATURE

> I am beginning to despair
> and can see only two choices:
> either go crazy or turn holy.
>
> **Adélia Prado, "Serenade"**

Sometimes the mystery of existence—that we exist at all, that we feel so homelessly at home in this place—gets embedded so deeply in life that we no longer feel it as mystery. Language, too, partakes of this sterilizing sameness, becomes in fact as solid and practical as a piece of wood or a pair of pliers, something we use during the course of interchangeable days. Poetry can reignite these dormancies ("words are fossil poetry," as Emerson put it), of both language and life, send a charge through reality that makes it real again.

I woke this morning so leaden I could hardly rouse myself from bed. I clutched for despair, but all the loyal life buoys—failure, self-contempt, God's "absence"—drifted out of reach. I felt . . . nothing, my whole being as solid and insentient as a piece of wood or a pair of pliers. (Hölderlin, going mad: "Nothing is happening to me, nothing is happening to me!") It was a teaching day, as unluck would have it: Gwendolyn Brooks, in a graduate divinity school seminar called Poetry and Faith. When I was a child, the two most intolerable aspects of my life (of which I was then conscious) were church and school. Both seemed to me so geologically dull I felt my arteries hardening. It seems either cold fate or high irony, then, that I should end up in church school. Some people can't conceive of a god who can't suffer. Me, I can't conceive of a god who can't laugh.

One wants a Teller in a time like this.

One's not a man, one's not a woman grown,
To bear enormous business all alone.

One cannot walk this winding street with pride,
Straight-shouldered, tranquil-eyed,
Knowing one knows for sure the way back home.
One wonders if one has a home.

One is not certain if or why or how.
One wants a Teller now: —

Put on your rubbers and you won't catch cold.
Here's hell, there's heaven. Go to Sunday School.
Be patient, time brings all good things—(and cool
Strong balm to calm the burning at the brain?)—
Behold, Love's true, and triumphs, and God's actual.

Gwendolyn Brooks, "The Womanhood"

When first reading this poem, one is likely to understand "Teller" as some sort of recorder or attentive onlooker. One wants a sensitive witness to capture and memorialize the "truth" of what happens "in a time like this." (The surrounding poems suggest war and social crisis, but specificity isn't needed; everyone alive has "a time like this.") But that reading quickly collapses. (That it was possible, though, lingers through and influences the rest of the poem.) What you want, actually, is a teller to tell you what you know is *not* true. Because in fact you are going to catch cold, bone cold, and hell and heaven are inextricable in this life, and time is ticking every instant toward a catastrophe orchestrated just for you.

But what about that last line? Is it merely a continuation of the wry irony of the first three lines of the stanza? Or does the parenthetical question, and the "cool strong balm" of its sound, chasten and change the tone, so that the "*Behold*" is credibly prophetic and annunciatory, not merely mockingly so? And if that word is credible and volatile in the ancient sense, then what of the assertions that follow?

"Actual" is a very precise word. A "telling" word, a crucial wingbeat away from the "real" that one might have expected. "Actual" comes to us from the Old French *actuel*, meaning "active, practical." Further back, the Latin *actus* meant "driving, doing, act or deed" (an *actus* was, literally, a cattle drive). Clearly the word once referred less to a condition than an action, less to a state of being than being itself. To say that God is actual, then, in the context of this poem, is not necessarily to say that God is "real." It's to say that God is so woven into reality that the question of God's own reality can't meaningfully occur.

One more pinhole precision: "and cool / Strong balm to calm the burning at the brain." "At," not the more expected "in." The burning is not psychological, or at least not entirely so, but circumstantial. The threat of meaninglessness is inside the speaker's mind, but it is a response to a threat that is external and palpable. The powers invoked by the poem—of telling (poetry), of love and God and patience—are not simply effective in the "real" world. They are what makes the world real. In the end, this is not a poem about

62

the reality of love, divinity, or poetry, but about the love, divinity, and poetry of reality.

Too much interpretation? Yes and no. Gwendolyn Brooks certainly never sat down and self-consciously seeded her poem with these meanings. My guess is she chose both "actual" and "at" entirely for the sounds (both of which are less predictable, less mellifluous). But that's the mystery of language, and of its reach into — rather, its coextensiveness with — life, love, and God. A reader's need can release a meaning an author never intended, but which her soul's submission to sound enabled. That's what happened for me in the midst of my barren dread this morning, and for the rest of the day love was true (from Old English, meaning "steadfast, loyal"), God was a verb (how lively and lovely the class!), and I was rescued by a revelation so tiny it would take a crazy and holy attention to see it as such.

12

SMART

At the pool club

He's smart. She's smart. It's Ivy all the way down.
That's Vlad, with his architectonic *r*'s and secular pecs,
who has learned the speech of trees or whatever.
And Astrid, our high-priestess of Post-postness,
ironizing infants, drizzling vinegar on the marzipan.
He's smart, she's smart, we carry our brains on little velvet pillows
we can never put down. I need three hands,
a woman with three doctorates and three chewing children
cheerfully avers. *Aver* is not a word one hears much these days,
the legal scholar avows, a breach of genre that costs him
three pairs of lowered eyes. Such tender, transgenic intelligences,
such minuscule and rococo meritocracies:
darling Sebastian, doing logic problems by the kiddie pool;
Margie-bear, scissor-kicking to a silent chaconne.
He's smart, she's smart, *Journalism*, we scoff as Sandra buoys by,
her two bestsellers bulging from her one-piece.
And Stuart! his own untenured ribs terror-taut,
his trunks notably bookless. We pause,
our eyes drawn skyward as for a rumble of thunder.
"As-tu lu le dernier Badiou?"
He's smart. She's smart. We know (our brains know)
muons from morons, apophatic from apoptosis,

stickleback mating tactics, Schengen currency shifts,
eighteenth-century Finnish hymnody, mit'a,
Ibn Fadlan and the Land of Darkness:
"If they see a man whose mind is lively and who knows many
   things, they say:
'This man deserves to serve our Lord.'
And they take him and put a rope round his neck and hang him
   in a tree
until he falls to pieces."

13

NO EPIPHANIES, PLEASE

I've never been in a gym I didn't like. Oh, there was the one in Paris where the machines were so close together you could taste your neighbor's *tartiflette*, and there was the stale room in far south Texas where, near as I could tell, I was the only member and worked out under the appraising gaze of a hard-bitten woman who couldn't keep herself from wondering how a man (she made the word include a question mark) had so much time for exercise. But even these were antidotes to despair.

It used to be that artists were allergic to exercise and relieved themselves with absinthe and orgies. Now there are spin classes. Not that I've ever attended a spin class, nor any other kind of group exercise. A good gym, like a good bar, fuses two things: oblivion and anonymity. Of course there are the ritual greetings and glances and such, but these should be minimal and strictly proscribed. The stack of towels should be so crisp and white they expunge all thought of other users. One should be able to run on a treadmill until one's mind is entirely erased.

Of course these are illusions. Exercise, like booze, can stave off reality only so long. But illusions are as essential to the good gym as they are to a democracy, and equally precarious. During the presidential race in 2016, one of my fellow gym-goers asked what I thought of Trump, and I immediately tore a spiritual tendon. What I love about gyms is their predictability, their moral clarity. Do this right and you are rewarded. Do it wrong and you are punished. *Trump? Here?* It was like discovering a slug in my oatmeal.

The gym I now belong to has codified this clarity. It describes itself as a "No Judgment Zone," and there are not only signs everywhere dissuading boorishness, but also an actual "Lunk Alarm" that goes off like an air-raid siren if the level of testosterone rises too high. I've heard it only once, and the poor Samson who set it off (by dropping his weights with a roar) seemed close to tears when he realized why all eyes were on him. (I have no idea who activates the thing—God probably.)

Every gym has its own elaborate taxonomy, and for many years this fascinated and enlivened me. The queens and the drones, the whippets and the peacocks. Nothing like decline to erode one's belief in distinctions. It's no wonder I've ended up in a gym that's mostly a lumpen mass of humanity, a gym that does not simply tolerate debacle and decrepitude but actively celebrates it. We are encouraged to enjoy a free piece of candy as we leave ("You've earned it!"), and once a week a large table is piled high with bagels and pizza.

For a brief time, though, a god dwelt among us. Tall, provocatively bald (you suspected a mane, I mean), chiseled as a cliff, he performed only two exercises. The first involved a pull-up bar and is beyond my powers of description. He alternated this with standing leaps onto a raised platform. That is to say, one minute he stood with an air of intense concentration, and then, with just a ripple in his skin like a breeze passing over still water, he materialized five feet higher in the air. Without a wobble. I've never seen anything like it, and judging from the way he disrupted the sludge, no one else had either. How I loved watching him; he made a whole different relation to exercise—and, somehow, to life—seem possible. And how glad I was when he was gone, for the same reason.

Predictability, anonymity, oblivion—again, these are the elements of a good gym. No epiphanies, please.

Which brings me face-to-face, as it were, with my final point: mirrors. These are, of course, ubiquitous in gyms, and for years I used them as everyone does, pretending to check out my form while checking out other unattainable things. Only lately have I realized the true focus and genius of this arrangement—as well as how much money it has saved me. "If a man stands before a mirror," writes Flann O'Brien, "and sees in it his reflection, what he sees is not a true reproduction of himself but a picture of himself when he was a younger man." This is, in my experience, correct. (And I suspect the specificity of the gender is damningly accurate.) But of late the self that has been ghosting the glass in front of me is not a man with pecs and purpose, nor even a man with, say, a bit of hair and decent knees. He's not a man at all, in fact, but a little boy of ten, back in 1976, which is when my daily exercise regimen began. I am certain of the date because *Rocky* came out that year and one morning I downed (like Rocky) and later upped (unlike Rocky) a tall glass full of raw eggs as part of my "training." I have forgotten the house we lived in at the time, can't recall a meal or holiday or even one word we said. Yet I remember every scent and sight of the predawn runs I began taking around the neighborhood, and the exact heft of my first plastic weights. A therapist would make much of this, no doubt, but obviously I don't need a therapist. I have a gym.

POSTSCRIPT

This little feuilleton appeared in *The New York Times Magazine* on March 18, 2020. Three days earlier—too late to stop the presses—all the gyms in New York were ordered closed because of Covid. The living began to seal themselves inside houses, and the dead began to fill up refrigerator trucks. The piece ran with an editorial note that read, to my ears, as part explanation, part apology, and part polite scream. I was embarrassed to have my name attached to the essay, though too immersed in my own urgencies to pay much attention (and in fact never saw the actual issue). In the following days, though, some readers reached out to me in ways that seemed incommensurate with the object that had prompted them, seemed eager to find some almost-spiritual meaning in the piece. If they noted the humor, it was mostly as a means of acknowledging an oceanic sadness upon which the tone, like a lonely buoy, bounces and floats.

I don't mean to make too much of this. It's a slight piece for a slight world, a little whistle in the instant before an earthquake. It did get me thinking again, though, about the spiritual dimensions of humor, how there can be, at times, an element of grace to it.

> Humor not only recognizes the comic discrepancy in the human condition, it also relativizes it, and thereby suggests that the tragic perspective on the discrepancies of the human condition can also be relativized. At least for the duration of the comic perception, the tragedy of man is bracketed.
>
> Peter Berger, A *Rumor of Angels*

I would say that our entire life is, in a sense, bracketed, and "religion reinterprets the meaning of the comic and vindicates laughter" (Berger again). Humor, in this reading, can be much more than mere comic relief (though, of course, it can sometimes be merely—and blessedly—that). It can have existential reach and significance, can imply a world in which the comic, not the tragic, is ultimate. Can imply it, at least, "for the duration of the comic perception." One must not breeze past that modest qualifier. As with a poem that restores reality to us and us to it, or a moment of joy that makes love seem not just possible but permanent, life (death) comes flooding back in with all its chaos and contempt for epiphanies, and the moment of "comic perception" can seem not just slight but irrelevant, even offensive. This can lead one to believe, like Thomas Hardy, that humor "is tragedy, if you only look deep enough into it." He means to subsume humor into tragedy, to make the latter more comprehensive and final than the former. Tragedy *is* more comprehensive and final than humor, in the same way that death, at least so far as we can tell, is more comprehensive and final than life. But I still think Hardy is wrong. Humor doesn't change its nature when submerged in tragedy. Like a vacancy defect, in which a missing atom actually makes a crystal stronger, a moment of humor can not only maintain its integrity but determine the strength and cohesion of the whole. Neither "vacancy" nor "defect" are the right words here, since what we are talking about is a superabundance of rightness. But the metaphor is apt enough. A comic perception can be not simply an act of faith, but a perdurable instant of time that faith itself can cling to—so long as that comic perception is, you might say, spiritually in tune with tragedy.

You won't believe this
—if you think you're reading a poem—
but someone just handed me a letter:
"I had dentures put in today,
and I do look younger,
but the old-person weariness persists."

And my terror vanished—
because in quoting the letter
I corrected two words,
and no one at the gates of hell
looks to grammar for help.
Thus once more I'm saved by a power,
a compassion
employing the constellations, the mail,
and the same mother tongue
that taught me to wail.

Adélia Prado, "The Good Shepherd"*

---

* On the other hand: "The Blues always impressed me as being very sad, sadder even than the Spirituals, because their sadness is not softened with tears, but hardened with laughter, the absurd, incongruous laughter of a sadness without even a god to appeal to." (Langston Hughes, from a letter to Carl Van Vechten)

KILL THE CREATURE

The infant shall play over the hole of the cobra,
and the young child dance over the viper's nest.

Isaiah, 11:8

I've always loved snakes. Love includes fear—for everyone, I think, but in the religious mind these emotions are married like grace and necessity, abundance and dearth. *Sanctify the Lord of hosts himself,* cries wise wild old Isaiah, *and let him be your dread.*

———

Recently I mentioned my lifelong fascination with snakes in the presence of my mother, who has perhaps the most—how to describe it exactly?—saturated, unmediated, sorrowful, solitary, and relentlessly religious mind that I know. Her faith has survived the violent deaths of her own parents in childhood, which she witnessed; and the violent rot of the one real romantic love she would ever know; and the inexplicable and inaccessible lives of her children, who have been homeless, and in prison, and drug addicts, and art addicts, and otherwise enamored of serpents. She flinched and objected as if I'd proclaimed a latent Satanism.

———

In childhood I would seek them out in the empty lots across from the apartment complex in Mesquite, or back of the train tracks in Brenham, or in the scrub that filled the gulch behind our house in Snyder, or in any of the other half dozen Texas towns that exist in me now as little more than random flashes and failures of memory. All these homeplaces, dreamplaces, doomplaces we carry around in our heads, as if the room were never quite right for the holy loneliness for which we seek both animation and ease.

———

The deepest being being a longing
to satisfy a longing for a solitude of two.

Lawrence Joseph, "That Too"

———

Why does one *create*? Two reasons: an overabundance of life and a deficiency of it; a sense that reality has called out in such a way that only your own soul can answer ("I create *in return*," said Robert Duncan) and a simultaneous sense that in that word "soul" is a hole that no creation of your own can ever quite fill. That long response that Job finally draws out of God, that blast of Arctic rhetoric — *Have you gone down to the springs of the sea / or walked in the unfathomable deep?* — what is this but the first form and final fruition, ratification and sharp rebuke, of all the poetry of loneliness? If there is consolation here, it is a cold one, a solidarity of starlight.

———

Kill the creature. That's practically the law where I grew up. Love has its sterner permutations, its "lonely and austere offices," an almost linguistic embeddedness in particular existence that precludes translation into another. *I love you*, the Father says to humanity as he assents again to humanity's endless need to annihilate him. *I love you*, I said to my father forty years ago with a fist to the side of his face. He—my father, I mean, or think I mean—is demented now and has just escaped again from another icy facility, each time by pretending to be the doctor that he in fact once was. Cunning man, deciding even the terms of his own dementia, carrying himself from place to place like a bag of stolen bones.

———

At an oil-field construction job I had one summer we worked for a month at a defunct refinery and every day laid the day's take out like a line of Italian eels for sale. Rattlesnakes, garter snakes, rat snakes, milk snakes, water snakes, lots of king snakes, thick and garish but completely harmless, helpful even, as they savor vermin. I remember two men tossing one of those whipping red-black serpents back and forth in the air like a live electric cord to see who was man enough to catch it. To calm it—as only one man could, gentling the creature to the point where it wrapped around his arm and practically licked his whiskers—until with a deft flick and flash its head spurted away from his sudden switchblade. (I also saw him do this—not the throwing part—with a rattlesnake that was coiled to strike.)

Then one morning I looked closely at one of the dull, dead king snakes and saw a band of yellow between the black and red, and when I pointed it out the foreman knew not the name but the rhyme that was meant to ward it off: *Red and yellow kill a fellow.*

It turned out to be a coral snake, the bite of which—because we were far from any hospital, and because coral snakes are extremely rare in west Texas and, unlike the other poisonous snakes around, require a very specific type of antivenom—would almost certainly have been fatal. I felt an excitement akin to sexual arousal, an almost spiritual joy. Was I realizing that this was part of my life now, this strange and vaguely dangerous story (though it seems pretty much impossible that those men played catch with this snake—probably it was severed by one of the big machines). Or did the excitement come from the realization that my life *was* a story, that I had some control over what seemed to me—my father vanishing, my mother wracked with rage and faith, my siblings sinking into drugs and alcohol, my own mind burning at night like an oil fire on water—complete chaos. Selves are nothing but memories of selves, and memories but the wispy entities that time and mind have conspired to keep. It's a wonder we don't walk through each other like ghosts.

———

The term "kenosis" refers to the kind of self-emptying that God performed both in the incarnation and the crucifixion. It is not in fact a "sacrifice" but a complete erasure for the sake of something greater. It is not reality but relationship that is greater. That is to say, it is not reality as we now know it, but the one we intuit at times by means of relationship—both with matter and with other minds. When God entered contingency, when the miracle of existence—that Being should be at all—became the bare, implacable fact of matter, there was no going back: either the incarnation is absolute, or it simply didn't happen. Either God is gone, or he never *was*.

In traditional Judeo-Christian religion—certainly the one I grew up in—the woman gets blamed for biting that apple of ultimate knowledge and bringing sin and death into the world. *Now the serpent was more subtle than any beast of the field which the Lord God had made. And he said unto the woman, Yea, hath God said, Ye shall not eat of every tree of the garden?* The misery this has engendered for women, the lives lost to the misunderstandings and manipulations of myth and how it means: in some ways a whole religion was wrecked on the shoals of a certain kind of mythological and poetic illiteracy that has only increased as we have matured in other ways:

> Woman is more guilty than man, because she was seduced by Satan, and so diverted her husband from obedience to God that she was an instrument of death leading to all perdition. It is necessary that woman recognize this, and that she learn to what she is subjected; and not only against her husband. This is reason enough why today she is placed below and that she bears within her ignominy and shame.

Thus John Calvin in the midst of the Protestant Reformation, which is what made the modern mind—its rationalism and individualism, its essential and lethal skepticism—possible. Thus the whole phalanx of unconsciously priapic preachers inveighing against the sweet disease that was gradually filling my adolescent body to bursting: woman. Just one taste and—*bam*—the end of Eden.

Which, at fifteen, was all I wanted. Even as the preachers poured down their fire on my head, all I could think of was the sweaty sex that first bite, because it was shared, must surely have led to, the momentary but complete release of it, how lewd and illicit and finally fucking free it must have been, how almost worth it, really, like the "free bloody birds" I would immediately recognize in Philip Larkin years later:

HIGH WINDOWS

When I see a couple of kids
And guess he's fucking her and she's
Taking pills or wearing a diaphragm,
I know this is paradise

Everyone old has dreamed of all their lives—
Bonds and gestures pushed to one side
Like an outdated combine harvester,
And everyone young going down the long slide

To happiness, endlessly. I wonder if
Anyone looked at me, forty years back,
And thought, *That'll be the life*;
No God any more, or sweating in the dark

About hell and that, or having to hide
What you think of the priest. He
And his lot will all go down the long slide
Like free bloody birds. And immediately

Rather than words comes the thought of high windows:
The sun-comprehending glass,

And beyond it, the deep blue air, that shows
Nothing, and is nowhere, and is endless.

Larkin's poem is ironic, of course: we all dream some freedom
we were ourselves denied. Or does this even happen anymore? I
can't imagine teenagers these days are any more sexually active or
inventive than they were among the eternal afternoons and tutorial
goats of Snyder, Texas. Even Larkin's poem concedes this, though
metaphysically rather than physically: Larkin's times did change,
though the meanings, or the meaninglessness — the ending image
is inexhaustibly provocative — did not. And what that image points
back to is Genesis itself: the Lord's face moving on the face of the
deep, glass that could comprehend the sun (that is, no separation
between mind and matter, e.g., scientific materialism, most mod-
ern poetry, all mysticism), some sheer clarity of existence that both
saves and rives you.

But, as I say, this all lay in wait for me. I didn't, couldn't imag-
ine the loneliness that must have come between Adam and Eve,
the selves they suddenly were — and thus forever weren't, quite. For
that's what Eve brought into the world, consciousness, or perhaps
more accurately the sin of separating consciousness from God.
The loneliness no human love can ever quite answer. And if you
are not lonely under this dividing and indifferent blue, if you do
not feel, even amid your moments of happiness, some absolute
inwardness that is absolute otherness, then, friend, you are either
preternaturally enlightened or completely unconscious.

But would you have it otherwise? Eve ought to get some credit
for bringing consciousness into existence, for the music and art and
poetry that have arisen from that rift; and for better — speculating
here, but it seems likely — sex; and then too the intricacies of atoms,
the impossibly immense cosmos, microbes and multiverses and all

that falls under the name of human knowledge, all the wonders wasted on atheists who must have their line in the sand, wasted on believers who do not have within them the hard unerring eye of the atheist that enables them to see that line in the sand—all this, too, we owe to a woman. Paradise is the purity no one ever wanted.

———

And anyway, paradise was poisoned from the start. "Cain, I will tell you a secret," says God to the first murderer in Howard Nemerov's poem "Cain": "I was the serpent in the Garden." "I can believe that," Cain says without pause or surprise,

> but nobody else will.
> I see it so well, that You are the master of the will
> That works two ways at once, whose action
> Is its own punishment, the cause
> That is its own result. It will be pain to me
> To reject You, but I do it, in Your own world,
> Where everything that is will speak of You,
> And I will be deaf.

As it happens, it's God who goes deaf in the poem, at least to the cries of Cain—which is to say, deaf to the cries of all of us. And it is Cain whose hearing grows only more excruciatingly acute:

> But He is gone, I feel His absence.
> As, after the storm's black accent,
> The light grows wide and distinct again,
> So He is gone. Of all He said to me,
> Only one thing remains. I send you away,

He said: Cain, I send you away.
But where is *Away*?

Precisely. Home and homelessness, election and rejection, autonomy and determinism, humanity and divinity: it's all one screaming weave. *If I had not come and spoken to them*, says God himself in one of the most disturbing and enlightening passages in the Bible (John 15:22), *they would not have sin.* The outraged objection here is obvious—God is a sadistic puppet master—and pointless. Some people can *think* their way to theories in which contingency and certainty are compatible terms (modern physicists, for example); a rarer few—mystics and artists, mostly—can on occasion actually *feel* it. ("Time violence rends the soul," says Weil, "by the rent eternity enters.") But in both instances the insight is partial and fugitive, disabling as well as enabling, because the flash of insight reveals a vastness no human insight will ever reach, and painful precisely because of how intimate that distance suddenly seemed. That intimate distance is God, in whom we move and live and have our being. Until we don't. We're all hunger artists of one sort or another, eating ourselves (our "selves") inward, trying to slake a hunger we usually can't even—or perhaps just won't dare to—name.

In the desert
I saw a creature, naked, bestial,
Who, squatting upon the ground,
Held his heart in his hands,
And ate of it.
I said, "Is it good, friend?"
"It is bitter—bitter," he answered;

"But I like it
"Because it is bitter,
"And because it is my heart."

Stephen Crane

———

According to Simone Weil, it is the self that separates us from God, and which we therefore must try to annihilate.

> We possess nothing in the world—a mere chance can strip us of everything—except the power to say "I." That is what we have to give to God—in other words, to destroy. There is absolutely no other free act which it is given us to accomplish—only the destruction of the "I."

> *Gravity and Grace*

There is a real truth here, but it is in a strange way distorted by the very clarity and austerity with which it is presented. Christianity teaches that we are to put others first, are to efface ourselves and our own needs. But to efface is not to erase, not completely; complete kenosis is possible only for God. In the end it's never quite clear to me what Weil means by the "self" unless it's simply every single thing that makes us human—or perhaps more accurately, every single thing that makes us *individually* human.

> The reality of the world is the result of our attachment. It is the reality of the self which we transfer into things. It has

nothing to do with independent reality. That is only perceptible through total detachment. Should only one thread remain, there is still attachment.

No way. If there is a reality distinct from our perception of it, there is no way we can reach it. This does not mean that we are all there is, each a king of infinite—and infinitely lonely—space. What it means is that reality is catalyzed by engagement, not detachment. John Keats intuited this in a letter of 1818, when he identified some aspects of reality that seemed to require a "greeting of the Spirit to make them wholly exist." In the two hundred years since, this bit of poetic intuition has come to a kind of physical fruition in science.

Most people are familiar with the double-slit experiment in which electrons behave as particles or waves depending upon whether someone is watching them. The physicist John Wheeler wondered what would happen if he observed the electrons after the fact of their having passed through a barrier. So instead of placing the register in front of the barrier, he placed it on the other side, *with exactly the same results*:

> The electrons seem to know in advance how the physicist will choose to observe them . . . The electron . . . is neither a wave nor a particle. It is in some sense unreal; it exists in an indeterminant limbo. "Not until you start asking a question, do you get something," Wheeler said. "The situation cannot declare itself until you've asked your question. But the asking of one question prevents and excludes the asking of another."

John Horgan, *The End of Science*

Where is an incarnate "God" in this scenario? What is the "self" and how does it stand in relation to God?

The word "God" becomes necessary where there is an intense feeling of presence and oneness in opposites, an awe that cannot let go of contradictory elements, of an otherness in which I am more truly "I."

Robert Duncan, *Collected Essays and Other Prose*

————

NATIVE

At sixteen,
sixteen miles

from Abilene
(Trent,

to be exact),
hellbent

on being not
this, not that,

I drove
a steamroller

smack-dab over
a fat black snake.

Up surged a cheer
from men

so cheerless
cheers

were grunts, squints,
whisker twitches

it would take
a lunatic acuity

to see.
I saw

the fat black snake
smashed flat

as the asphalt
flattening

under all ten tons
of me,

flat as the landscape
I could see

no end of,
flat as the affect

of distant killing
vigilance

it would take a native
to know was love.

———

To attend is to atone. There is no looking at reality "straight up,"
so to speak. "The mathematical descriptions of the physical world
given to us by quantum theory presuppose the existence of observ-
ers who lie outside those mathematical descriptions," writes the
physicist Stephen Barr. In other words, there is nowhere to stand in
order to be outside of what you are examining, for the object of ob-
servation is changed by the act of observation. Every gesture toward
absolute human knowledge reaches right back to and with that first
hand grabbing the apple. Even our equations implicate us.

   This is not news, I realize. It is thought to be a discovery of the
modern era, from Nietzsche's famous "There are no facts, only in-
terpretations," right on through the physical confirmations of this
statement from modern physics. But as usual, science has simply
confirmed what poets and proper theologians always—"knew," I
was going to say, but that would be wrong, unless knowing is al-
ways alert to the ultimate truth that it cannot know any ultimate
truth, including the one this sentence is attempting to articulate.
This is the ouroboros, the snake with its tail in its mouth. There
is nowhere to stand and *see*, nowhere to escape the stink of being
human. To attend is to atone.

———

           what the eye flies after trans-
                   luces; what
        you want, doesn't want: it vanishes . . .

you're only yours, mutter and
muscles, as you enter it, its vanishing.

Gustaf Sobin, "Shadow Rattles"

Gustaf Sobin (1935–2005) was a little-known American poet who spent most of his adult life in an abandoned silk cocoonery in Provence trying to respond to a call that he could neither identify nor escape. It's a common dilemma for modern artists. ("What could I call what was calling me?" writes Fanny Howe. "A vocation that has no name.") Sobin, who adhered to no particular religion, believed that divinity had "undergone eclipse" and thought of a line of poetry as a "traced erasure." Contrary to modern psychology, articulating a dilemma does not always ease the anguish:

> What hasn't vanished, however, is the need—call it psychic imperative—that such an address exists. Long after the addressee has vanished, after the omniscient mirror has dissolved and its transcendent dimension has been dismantled, demystified, deconstructed, there remains that psychic imperative deeply inscribed within the innermost regions of our being. We can't do, it would seem, without something that isn't.

Indeed we can't. Nor could Meister Eckhart, a Christian mystic who died nearly seven hundred years before Sobin: "Only the hand that erases can write the true thing." Nor could Saint Paul, who was a contemporary of Jesus himself:

> But God hath chosen the foolish things of the world to confound the wise; and God hath chosen the weak things of the world to confound the things which are mighty;

And base things of the world, and things which are de-
spised, hath God chosen, yea, *and things which are not, to
bring to nought things that are.*

1 Corinthians 1:27–28

The italics are mine, but the existential anguish—and the faith
that makes that anguish not simply bearable but even joyful—is all
Paul. We can't do without something that isn't.

———

Another summer, another job, we drained a tank and my task, be-
cause I was a miserable menial high school student, was to trudge
through the bottom-muck in thigh-high waders, spearing the spir-
ited creatures that thrashed and slithered as if the earth itself were
acquiring primordial form and violent volition. I remember this,
but can it be true? What snakes would have been down there? Water
snakes, cottonmouths, I suppose—but such an infernal tangle? It
seems unlikely from this distance. What stands out as incontrovert-
ible fact is the sudden, massive, mud-covered reptile sliced in half
by a backhoe, writhing its red stub of blood in the air like a giant's
arm severed at the shoulder.

———

My father lost half of his foot to an adolescent rattler coiled
in the bushes under his window in the ranch house where he
lived outside Fort Worth. He was drunk and had locked himself
outside. Thus the window. He was wearing only gym shorts and
a T-shirt and had simply wanted to sit out on his porch while

the sun went down. He had no phone, no wallet, no hidden spare key.

My father is a man in whom life thrives as a form of death. There is a cancerous élan to him, a mind of maggots that have learned to eat with just such modest ferocity as will keep their host alive. A few years ago, though, he began "failing to thrive," a term I thought existed only for infants until the hospice workers, who will take over only when a person's end is imminent, told me otherwise. He withered to 140 pounds (he is six feet tall), never left bed, and eventually refrained from all speech excepting sudden floods of psychotic invective and rage. There was no medical reason for the catastrophe that was clearly taking place inside of this sixty-nine-year-old man. It seemed, like everything else about him, willful. *Failure* to thrive had it exactly backward.

It's a matter of days, they said, as his organs began to shut down. *It can't be long now*, as they removed the feeding tube and discontinued all treatments that were not palliative in nature. I was there for a twenty-four-hour period and he never moved a muscle, never opened an eye. *Then said Jesus unto him, Except ye see signs and wonders, ye will not believe.* One morning he stood up. One morning while everyone waited for his last breath, he got out of bed completely naked, tore the tubes out of his arm, and told everyone to get the fuck out of his house.

———

He sucked the venom from his foot the best he could, fashioned a tourniquet out of his T-shirt (both of which only exacerbated the problem) and made his way to the highway, which was about two hundred yards away. But because he was barefoot and thus subject to glass and stickers and what have you, and because the venom was rapidly making its way through his bloodstream, he was soon crawling and increasingly delirious. It is preferable to be bitten by an enormous old rattlesnake rather than a small young one, for the old snake has learned something of miraculous chance and venomous contingency, and it usually will not discharge its entire hoard. A young snake simply lets fly.

———

Just think how very old Satan must have been, even in Eden— though I suppose if we think of time beginning with the creation of the cosmos, and if we allow the myth to speak of that moment, then he was in his way every bit as young and even innocent as Eve. Are we then—humanity, I mean—suffering from a judicious dose to which the right antidote may yet be found, or has it all been one long strangling cry of dying?

———

There is a moment in the life of a writer when one ceases to care about the truth as if there were any sort of abstract objective word or occurrence that could warrant that name. I don't mean one loses fidelity to the facts. I believe one should hew to the facts as one remembers them, even as it seems scientifically incontrovert-ible that memory is mostly an act of imagination. The ouroboros again.

No, what I mean has to do with *meanings*, or the lack thereof. It's not that I don't believe in them anymore, it's that I believe they are ultimately unknowable, even the most intimate aspects of our existence, including the mutilations that made us what we are.

One follows the sounds. One follows them obsessively, religiously, if religion can be understood as having no sponsor, no ultima Thule, no final ground of meaning, which is *not* to say no God. ("Only the hand that erases can write the true thing.") One wants only the cadences to continue as if there were something in the words themselves that sought meaning—sought concretion, even—out there in the world, or something out there in the world that corresponded so intimately and utterly to the sounds of the words that the intensity and gravity of one particular existence—or even one moment within that existence—might catalyze the tongues in trees, books in the running brooks, sermons in stones, and every evil thing.

———

Including the mutilations that made us what we are. It's a direct quote from the American philosopher Richard Rorty, and it's from a footnote to a little dialogue he had with the Italian theologian Gianni Vattimo called *The Future of Religion*. Rorty, an American pragmatist who did not believe in God (Rorty died in 2007), and Vattimo, an Italian Catholic who believes that all essential questions about God are unanswerable and therefore irrelevant, discover much common ground. If you find yourself hungering for something more than the "social cooperation" that, according to Rorty, the combination of modern science and common sense can offer, "then a religion that has been taken out of the epistemic arena, a religion that finds the question of theism versus atheism uninteresting, may be just what suits your solitude."

Patronizing? Perhaps just a bit, but Vattimo serenely, if insidiously, agrees: "Things appear to us in the world," he writes, "only because we are in their midst and always already oriented toward seeking a specific meaning for them." (Keats!) Then Vattimo carries this logic to its natural conclusion: "Can we really argue, as I believe we must, that postmodern nihilism constitutes the actual truth of Christianity?" I have mentioned this quote to some religious people I know and every time their faces fall, but I can't tell you how freeing I find the idea, because it accords so precisely with my own experience, which sometimes seems to be both animated and annihilated by nothingness. "Nihilism," though, is not at all the right word, as it suggests an assertiveness and stasis that elsewhere Vattimo clearly refutes. "The meaning of Christianity as a message of salvation consists above all in dissolving the peremptory claims of 'reality.'" And from a different book, *Belief* (the literal and much more revelatory translation of the original title is *I Believe That I Believe*): "Christ himself is the unmasker; and . . . the unmasking inaugurated by him . . . is the meaning of the history of salvation itself."

Thus the old language, as well as the dynamic it enacts (redemption, salvation) is recovered and restored—not with any metaphysical assurance and certainly not permanently, as the next age will have to remake and reimagine (and, as the quotes from Eckhart and Paul reveal, recover) its own language for faith. But there is a kind of smelling-salt shock and astringency to such an approach, a recognition that, as physics has shown us, we cannot know the world independent of ourselves, but within such vertiginous existence, knowing that we do not know, the next step becomes possible. Myth and metaphor reacquire their kinship with the unconscious, and the dark matter (a metaphor, note) of reality becomes, instead of corrosively unknowable, the very terrain of faith. Poetry is the only sanity.

———

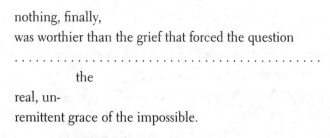

nothing, finally,
was worthier than the grief that forced the question

. . . .

      the

real, un-
remittent grace of the impossible.

Gustaf Sobin, "Shadow Rattles"

After the second of my father's four wives died, he and I went to East Africa to visit her missionary daughter and son-in-law. I have written of this elsewhere. I have written of all of this elsewhere in one way or another because let me tell you any writer who claims writing is a calling and not an obsession is either blessed or afflicted with youth or dementia. I have been addicted to opiates in my life and I must say that there is a kinship between that flood of sane and aimable elation that opiates engender and the release of meaning when the right sounds are linked together.

Notice I do not put meaning in quotes here. I'm a Christian. Which means that I have faith. Or had it once, and with such enlivening force that to deny it now would be a denial of life itself. ("All I do is try to stay on the side of belief," says a priest in Fanny Howe's novel *Indivisible*.) *What is truth?* says postmodern Pilate to the man whose life has suddenly called everything into question. Christ crucified is not the answer to that question, but a call and catalyzing means to act upon it.

They—the missionaries—went to immense trouble to get their black Lab, Brandy (an innocent naming, I feel quite sure—a spiritless one, let us say), shipped first to Europe for a few weeks and then to

Nairobi and then trucked over the Serengeti to the impoverished and ramshackle city in far western Tanzania where they lived. Lived happily, I should say, all eight of them, with their home-grown butter beans and their motorcycles, their drawling Swahili and inflexible fundamentalisms, their abashing acts of charity and unselfconscious compassion, their many multicolored lizards that every night crawled down the walls into their names. Alfie, Little Peep, Shanga-shanga.

How happy they—again, the missionaries—were the day of that dog's arrival. It was beautiful domestic ecstasy, the children all bounding around the yard, the dog lost in an orgy of olfactory intoxications. Well of course you know where this is going. You with your secular distance and savviness, your ironized idealisms, you who think what the fuck do they think they're doing anyway, these rubes, bringing the false balm of God to bear upon these ferociously real wounds. You. Suddenly from under a corner of the porch leaps the black mamba your own mind has made, and the children, delicately schooled in loss by the months of Brandy's absence, are now in stern session.

———

I remember eating rattlesnake at some fair somewhere—Fort Worth, probably, Weatherford, Sweetwater, who knows. Inch-thick slabs toothpicked on a platter someone must have served. I was six or seven. My parents were separated again, and my mother was surviving by taking in boarders, all of whom had growling Harleys and cigarette-smelling beards and huge black boots. My mother has no memory of this—the particular boarders—so here we go round the rattlesnake again. It tasted like chicken. Of course it did.

Live long enough and even memory begins to taste like chicken. Or rattlesnake.

———

It was a young couple who finally stopped in the darkness—for it had become quite dark—to help my father. What a brave pair of people, pulling over in the dark and then not racing away at the sight of this hairy hell-bound hallucinating ogre on his knees like some insane supplicant. Nothing is more terrifying, more viscerally repulsive, than the animal will for survival, that creature more creature than we are, who will eat razor wire and lick shit from jackboots if he has to, that maw of meaningless breathing down which, when the real crisis of survival comes, our "self" is sucked like vegetable cuttings roared down the disposal.

(But this sort of self-destruction, according to Weil, does not work. Is too late. The self that is destroyed from the outside rather than from the inside is subject only to degradation and humiliation, an erasure that raises nothing in its wake. *Whosoever shall fall upon that stone shall be broken,* says Jesus, *but on whomsoever it shall fall, it will grind him to powder.*)

How did it play out? Did she want to stop and he didn't, or was it the reverse? And was it goodness or guilt, or the two raveled too closely together to separate? Or did they simply stop without a word because they were Christians, and to be a Christian is to know that "the only truth revealed to us by Scripture, the one that can never be demythologized in the course of time—since it is not an experimental, logical, or metaphysical statement but a call to practice—is the truth of love, of charity" (Vattimo again). That's the only explanation the doctors gave, that the people, whom we

94

never met, and who left no names, had described themselves as Christians.

———

There remain the snakes. Lying like animate mud or coagulations of creek water straight and sun-glutted on the concrete spillway spilling just a little trickle of runoff just this side of drought. The creek is Barton Springs, and in a few months it will rise up like the fountains of the deep and trap me at the ranch for ten days. But now it is midmorning, south Texas, 1994, and I have come to a three-hundred-acre ranch to be alone for six months to work on a poem. I know. It makes me smile to think of it, too, though at least now I am able to feel some affection for the confusedly devout and overserious self that I was. It was a worthy expenditure of life, whatever the results. And also the long and anything-but-lazy afternoons when I read Proust and Shakespeare, every word of each, shouting sometimes to the errant longhorns that had jumped the five-foot fence (who knew a cow could jump like that?):

> She loved me for the dangers I had passed,
> And I loved her that she did pity them!

And occasionally there were weekend visitors, like my father and his third wife, both of whom, the very first time we were crossing the creek, suddenly pulled out pistols and began firing methodically into water that, they swore, had a minute before been the most massive snake.

But mostly I was there to finish a poem, one long poem that went to the heart of what I heard like a little trickle of bedraggled rainwater in my brain, way-back water from my family's origins in ruin that was real and thus, I sensed, redemptive. By "real" I mean ruin that has metaphysical status. I mean suffering that is, if not ordained, at least contained within an apprehensible arena of action and consequence, affliction and redemption. I mean something in which I had no faith but for the faith in language that led me on.

And leads me on. Here, now, decades later, creeping through the ordinary midmorning light of my own mind in search of snakes. They are always there if it is hot, just up from the water basking where the dirt road turns to concrete, at least three or four, sometimes eight or ten—and they always know that I am coming. I tiptoe down toward the water, trying to be so comprehensively gone that their seismographic skins and trip-wire tongues that sense everything will sense, for once, nothing. But even frozen I must breathe. Even out of sight I am in the sleepy eons of their brains as they melt back into the mud, deliquesce in the dirty water I would not, will not, cannot for the life of me wade into now.

———

But as I rav'd and grew more fierce and wilde
    At every word,
Methought I heard one calling, *Child!*
    And I reply'd, *My Lord*.

George Herbert, "The Collar"

———

Here's how it ends. Once, driving with a woman going mad, I stopped to see a snake. It was on a hot back road in a dead flat place and we whipped right over it though I could see—no, I *knew*—that it had been entirely untouched. It reared up defiantly in the middle of the road and stared at us—at me, as I was the one getting out of the car and advancing toward it despite the tremulous protests of the woman who was going mad. "Going mad" is perhaps not fair or accurate, as it implies a drama and energy she entirely lacked. Say that two years earlier a scintilla of intolerable sorrow had entered her like a drop of ink in water, and now night was almost all she was. Kill the creature, I thought to myself on that hot blacktop, which is odd since I am essentially the opposite of the wanton boy I was and now can't bring myself to kill a spider in the house. I gave the snake—a rat snake, a black snake, an anonymous and everywhere kind of snake—a little nudge with my foot to get it moving off of the road, but it only angered and tried to strike me. So I stood for a second staring out at the eternal, infernal fields of my childhood, then went back to the car and the woman who would shortly endure every amalgam of abrasive chemical astringents that would do no good, and radical electroshock that would do no good, and prayer that would do no good. She was huddled in the passenger seat whimpering something softly to herself. What could I say? To attend is to atone? Nihilism constitutes the actual truth of Christianity? *I'm sorry*, I said to the windshield, and to the woman going mad, and to the child I had not realized was so immanent in me that it was he who had insisted I get out of that car, he who stood over that harmless black snake gently touching it with his tennis shoe, he who stopped and stared out at the god-shocked wasteland with a gaze so reciprocally blank it would take a native to know it was love.

ARS POETICA

I.

—a plum and othering dusk,
something renunciatory in the light,
until the sparrow takes the old tree's shape
and the trees untreed are everywhere.

If I could let go
If I could know what there is to let go
If I could chance the night's improvidence
and be the being this hard mercy means.

II.

These lost and charnel thoughts
less thoughts than bits of stun
I suddenly find myself among;

that are the me I am when I am not
sleeked to reason and pacific despair
speak to me of a pain that saves,

some endmost ear to shrive the mind.

FAITH COMES THROUGH HEARING

Some days, although we cannot pray, a prayer
utters itself. So, a woman will lift
her head from the sieve of her hands and stare
at the minims sung by a tree, a sudden gift.

Some nights, although we are faithless, the truth
enters our hearts, that small familiar pain;
then a man will stand stock-still, hearing his youth
in the distant Latin chanting of a train.

Pray for us now. Grade 1 piano scales
console the lodger looking out across
a Midlands town. Then dusk, and someone calls
a child's name as though they named their loss.

Darkness outside. Inside, the radio's prayer—
Rockall. Malin. Dogger. Finisterre.

Carol Ann Duffy, "Prayer"

"Faith comes through hearing." I always think of that line from the
apostle Paul (Romans 10:17) when I read—or rather hear, for this
poem only comes fully to life out loud—this "prayer." Spreading
the Gospel is Paul's concern—"How can they believe in the one

99

of whom they have not heard?"—but as is often the case with scripture, some charged, less teachable truth has infiltrated the lesson. Faith comes, in this deeper sense, not through taking in and assimilating the meaning of words, not through content at all, at least not primarily. It comes, literally, from the air, from sound. I would say it's pre-Christian if Christianity didn't itself contain its own cosmic origin and extinction: *"In the beginning was the Word, and the Word was with God, and the Word was God."* I say "origin" because the verse puts Christ not simply at the beginning of creation but as its source and means of sustenance. (God *speaks* existence into being in Genesis.) And I say "extinction" because every human utterance exists in the shadow of—and is annihilated in the full light of—that divine one. You can't hear the word of God until you've heard the Word of God. The word is imparted, the Word intuited. The word comes from a minister, of whatever sort (a poet, say). The Word might come from the leaves of a tree, or a rudimentary piano lesson, or a radio's shipping forecast.

Sound, then, that's the first thing to attend to in poems. And what a sound this solemn sonnet makes. It's so beautiful, in fact, so consolingly clear and assured, that you might not notice the enormous gulfs of despair and unbelief it has carried you over. There is a sense of volatile melancholy in the poem—is the woman with her head in her hands praying or grieving?—a sorrow just on the verge of revelation. ("The knowledge of the fallen world does not kill joy," writes Alexander Schmemann, "which emanates in this world, always, constantly, as a bright sorrow.") And then that sorrow becomes more explicit: "someone calls / a child's name as though they named their loss." The pain of childhood, even if it's just the sense of its end, gets healed over by time until one day you find yourself with your own child, whose presence gives you so much joy that it jolts loose a sadness—a wound—you'd forgotten: and you call your child's name as though you named your loss. The "truth" that enters your heart is restorative and necessary but it is also a "small familiar pain." W. H. Auden once defined poetry as the clear expression of mixed feelings. The truth of this poem is small and familiar and deeply consoling, but it is also pain.

"Prayer" ends with those place names from the shipping forecast, as if the very earth cried out to God, as indeed it does sometimes in scripture. Which is precisely the point: some days, although we cannot pray—because we are too busy, or because we are in too much pain, or simply because the words will not come—a prayer utters itself. There is a wrenching moment near the end of Marilynne Robinson's novel *Lila* when the title character and her husband, John Ames, are discussing, almost arguing, issues of faith and prayer. Ames finally throws up his arms and says, "Family is a prayer. Wife is a prayer. Marriage is a prayer." By which he means to say something similar to what Carol Ann Duffy is saying in her poem, that the world and the soul, our existence and God's, are far more permeable—and much more *possible*—than words like "faith," "truth," or even "prayer" can suggest.

17

FLASHBACK

Last night D. came home after three days away and the girls were so animated and irrepressible it was as if a stitch had slipped and all the withheld stress came singing through the seams of them as joy. A difficult joy: how one girl had bitten the other after a disagreement about the proper length of my hair in a sidewalk chalk drawing; how they'd decided to decorate the handmade dining room table with their paints; or how, when I'd suggested we bring one of the tiny robin hatchlings into the house, Eliza said—without irony, or with an unconscious irony she has suckled from the atmosphere of us—"Why, so you can write a poem about it?" But still: joy. At dinner outside, when D. had gone for more food, Eliza said as the door closed that she'd been scared that Mommy wasn't ever going to come back, and then she turned to me exclaiming, "My heart would just split into nothing and wouldn't even be a heart anymore." Which is what I told D. later lying in bed, after we had gone through all the details of our respective days. There was no need to acknowledge the content of the silence that ensued—the hard blast of chemo I had received in the fall, the four pneumonias that followed—nor the familiarity and solidarity with which we moved past it. I suppose every real intimacy includes its end—and not as a concept either, not as a realization or focus, not a third thing upon which two people might focus their gazes instead of directly at each other—like art, like children. No, the end inhabits every authentic act and word, and the final silence that so pains love is the same silence that sustains love. In other words, the knowledge of love and the knowledge of death are the same, and neither is knowledge.

[18]

SO IT BE OURS

Love is lak de sea. It's uh movin' thing, but still and all, it takes its shape from de shore it meets, and it's different with every shore.

Zora Neale Hurston, *Their Eyes Were Watching God*

Loving each other began this way: threading
loneliness into loneliness
patiently, our hands trembling and precise.

Yehuda Amichai, "Threading"

When deception and truth are presented as two equal possibilities in contrast to each other, the decision is whether there is love or mistrust in you. For example, one says, "Even what appears to be the purest feeling can nevertheless be a deception—certainly it is possible; it must be possible— *ergo* I choose mistrust or belief in nothing."

Søren Kierkegaard, *Works of Love*

Two thoughts were so mixed up I could not tell
Whether of her or God he thought the most,

But think that his mind's eye,
When upward turned, on one sole image fell;
And that a slight companionable ghost,
Wild with divinity,
Had so lit up the whole
Immense miraculous house
The Bible promised us,
It seemed a gold-fish swimming in a bowl.

W. B. Yeats, "All Souls' Night"

Marriage
is an exercise
in watching another
lose—one grows
attuned—
soon, you can
distinguish between the
instance of
severance—
how pain enters
their face
like a hand hunting
inside a
puppet—and the
moment they
understand
they're now empty
as a sock.

Katie Farris, "Marriage, an Exercise"

because when what has become dormant,
meager or hardened
passes through the electric

of you, the fugitive scattered pieces
are called back to their nature—
light pouring through muslin

in a strange, bare room.

August Kleinzahler, "Land's End"

Time reigns; yet the kingdom of love is every moment,
Whose citizens do not age in each other's eyes.

Vernon Watkins, "Taliesen and the Spring of Vision"

It was as if they had leapt over the arduous calvary of con-
jugal life and gone straight to the heart of love. They were
together in silence like an old married couple wary of life,
beyond the pitfalls of passion, beyond the brutal mockery
of hope and the phantoms of disillusion: beyond love. For
they had lived together long enough to know that love was
always love, anytime and anyplace, but it was more solid the
closer it came to death.

Gabriel García Márquez, *Love in the Time of Cholera*

Let grief
Be
So it be ours

George Oppen, "Anniversary Poem"

D., GARDENING

One form of matter completed by grief.
One psalm so utter its form is life.

One fire further than the one in which we've burned.
One world more than our wounds have earned.

One love so lavish it is not one.
You look up, love, for a time entirely sun.

LEOPARD BREATHES AT LAST!

It might be lonelier
Without the Loneliness—
I'm so accustomed to my Fate—
Perhaps the Other—Peace—

Would interrupt the Dark—
And crowd the little Room—
Too scant—by Cubits—to contain
The Sacrament—of Him—

Emily Dickinson, #405

A quixotic notion. "Peace," which I take to be the peace of God,*
would "interrupt the Dark" that, one assumes, has in the past made
God possible. Though the rest of the poem seems to say that the
room was always too small to contain that presence. In any event,
loneliness is both condition and companion here, as in one of
Fanny Howe's novels when a character is said to be "dead of God."

———

* Though I suppose another reading is possible—the peace of another person's pres-
ence, human love; though see entry number fourteen for a sense of how those two
things—for me, and I think deep down for Dickinson—are ultimately indistinguishable.

I think of Dickinson as the poet of aboriginal loneliness, her ear tuned to the timelessness when God's own loneliness (yes), with one cry (I think of it as a cry) created and evacuated matter. "Loneliness," writes Yehuda Amichai, "is one of the tenses in which an action's time can be conjugated." *Now* it is:

> Inquisitor! incognizable Word
> Of Eden and the enchained Sepulchre,
> Into thy steep savannahs, burning blue,
> Utter to loneliness the sail is true.

Hart Crane, "Ave Maria"

———

To be irremediably unhappy—this is shameful. An irremediably unhappy person is outside the laws of earth. Any connection between him and society is severed finally. And since, sooner or later, every individual is doomed to irremediable unhappiness, *the last word of philosophy is loneliness.*

Lev Shestov, *All Things Are Possible*

———

"Because he was lonely he became a theologian," wrote Dietrich Bonhoeffer's closest friend Eberhard Bethge, "and because he became a theologian he was lonely." The trivial reading of this statement is, firstly, that God, for Bonhoeffer, was compensatory, a stopgap he turned to when life could not meet his expectations; and secondly, that it's a lonely business being a theologian because (a) there aren't many of them and (b) no one cares. As I say, trivial. What Bethge is trying to express is that Bonhoeffer became a theologian because he sensed that his primal loneliness had its origin and end in God, and because he gave his life over to this pursuit, he became in some way unfit for ordinary happiness. This didn't turn him into a glumhound. In fact he was by all accounts buoyant and vital, a bit of a dandy, and in his last years a source of great spirit and succor to the fellow prisoners with whom he suffered. But he was lonely in a way that only God eases, and he was Christian in a way that knows that God, insofar as he is fully Christ and thus fully human, never quite does (never quite can?). To put it differently, loneliness is a condition that God both eases and is.

———

"Because he was lonely he became a theologian, and because he became a theologian he was lonely." I keep wanting to replace "theologian" with "poet."

———

In any event, this is a dynamic—and a hard truth—that the "religiously unmusical" mind (to quote Max Weber) does not understand; or that the contemporary conservative religious mind, with its (laudable) emphasis upon an intimate personal relationship with God, has either repressed or transcended; or that liberal Protestantism has effectively muted with its (laudable) emphasis on community and social justice; or that the neoorthodox strand of Christianity, with its (laudable) emphasis on the absolute otherness of God, has resigned itself to under the guise of triumph (Karl Barth); or that I and a few cold souls suffer alone. Because not only am I convinced that there is a lifting energy, an answering appeal and promise, in precisely this most interior ice of human loneliness, which no human love can ever quite crack, but I am also convinced—no, I cling to the notion, I ache acutely with the vaguest of aims and strain to call it faith—that there is in human love both a plea for, and a promise of, the love of God.

―――――

Loneliness, as Shestov says, may be the last word of philosophy. But it's the first word of faith. And what is the last word of faith? Love.

―――――

With thee, in the Desert—
With thee in the thirst—
With thee in the Tamarind wood—
Leopard breathes—at last!

Dickinson, #209

112

THE DRIFT OF THE WORLD

I.

Sometimes it seems there's nothing left to read. Nothing new, I mean. In English, I mean, which is the only language I read well enough to read with my ear (that is to say, with my soul). Of course I come across striking individual poems here and there, and of course the old favorites remain mercurial and volatile and always have some new shadow to enlighten me. But I long for that bracing, immersive shock of style, the infiltration of an entire consciousness that both unsettles and restores my own, rather than the detached admiration of some singular aspect. I am fifty-three years old and have somehow never before read—or, more accurately, never properly *heard*—William Bronk.

MIDSUMMER

A green world, a scene of green, deep
with light blues, the greens made deep
by those blues. One thinks how
in certain pictures, envied landscapes are seen
(through a window maybe) far behind the serene
sitter's face, the serene pose, as though
in some impossible mirror, face to back,

human serenity gazed at a green world
which gazed at this face.
                    And see now,
here is that place, those greens
are here, deep with those blues. The air
we breathe is freshly sweet, and warm, as though
with berries. We are here. We are here.
Set this down, too, as much
as if an atrocity had happened and been seen.
The earth is beautiful beyond all change.

It's not as if this comes out of nowhere. Wallace Stevens is the obvious antecedent, as many people have pointed out. But Stevens is garish and flickering and rampant. Bronk is muted, focused, subdued. Stevens is the consummate fox, inspiration blazing in a million different directions. Bronk is all hedgehog. He knows one thing, which is that he does not truly know one thing. He sometimes seems determined *not* to be inspired.

But one almost gives up on this poem before that memorable end. The repetition and imprecision, the numb adjectives ("sweet," "warm") that actually haze the scene they supposedly refine—it all seems almost complacently vague. Then the poem stabs your soul. It's an odd effect: the physical description in this poem feels abstract, whereas the abstraction feels concrete. This is not, in fact, an effect but a vision of reality, which for Bronk is, no matter how immediately acute, ultimately untouchable. ("'Well, of course,' he said, 'we take a different approach / to reality.' As though it were something that lay / like a lump in the yard, that anyone could kick.") The last lines of "Midsummer" don't memorialize—and may not even refer to—some actual event in the poet's life but instead resonate into life itself. One sees the sound, as it were.

"Ideas are always wrong," Bronk says in a poem that is an idea, in a book that is itself so abstract it's like some Platonic library, a library in which there is one book, one person (you; Bronk is not there), one tone that has no more range than the hum of the fluorescent lighting.

> Of lovers, one senses how, coupled, their joy is to think
> their singleness, together, to find themselves;
> how, holding each other, they think to hold
> as well as themselves, the truth, reality.
>
> We honor their wanting; what better could we want than that?
> Or, more than honor, we feel what they feel.
> If not for another sense, then this were all:
> we sense that what they hold is not the truth.

"The Holding"

Truth. It's a word that haunts even the poems in which it doesn't appear. Like a lot of modern poets, Bronk's intuition clashes with his intellect. He is driven toward a unity and finality of perception that his poems—and presumably his life—keep telling him does not exist. He feels what he cannot believe in. He will not resolve this clash with a reverberating image or epiphany, a celebration of the everlasting everyday. The "everyday," in fact, is scoured out of Bronk. There is something ruthless, swoonless, comfortless, something just plain *less*, about this voice. I am put in mind of an advertisement that ran many years ago in which we see a seared and desiccated man crawling out of a desert into a town. When the townspeople gather above him, the only words the man can manage to whisper are, "Give me some potato chips."

III.

> They come home. They come back. They find their way to us.
> Sniffing. Nudging our legs with their noses. They are ours.
> Whose should they otherwise be? They curl content.
> Discarded animals we thought we could lose
> by losing them. Damn them! Here they are.
>
> **"Euclidean Spaces: Linear Time"**

> Let me not have a life to look at, the way we look
> at a life we build to look at, in the world belief
> gives us to understand, a snowman life.
>
> **"On *Credo Ut Intelligam*"**

> She wants me to say something pretty to her because
> we both know the unabettable
> bleak of the world. Make believe, she says,
> what harm? It may be so. I can't. I don't.
>
> **"The Inability"**

IV.

We become more susceptible to, more partial to, the abstract as we get older. This is not because of increased understanding or any onset of wisdom, nor is it the result of diminished intensity. It's often just the opposite. The particular is too much for us, because it is leaving us.

Is that right? Or is it that the particular is too much for us, because there is too much of it? Who could guess that all the fires and despairs of youth, all those almost intolerable nows, would eventually pile up in a mass of time too obdurate and undifferentiated to be called memory? Or, worse, that some present-day gale of pain or need might cause that mass of losses—for that's what, at this point, they are—to disperse and go swirling around you with a force that no form, much less a mind, could contain. It can be a relief to release one's hold on singularity for the sake of a binding truth, even if the truth is only that there can be no such thing. If we can't salvage the bits of memory and matter that have made us what we are, let us at least acknowledge the whirlwind.

So many things happen; many smaller than a sparrow's fall.
It is a long rain in rain country where the flow
falls steadily all day and all night long
and the next day keeps on falling in an air
half air, half water, and a world half gone
to dissolution, fluid and almost formless
in the rain of small occurrences. So many things happen
at a single time, it seems an idleness
to note them all, or try to note them all,
for who could note them, smaller than a sparrow's fall.

"The Rain of Small Occurrences"

For Bronk it's impossible that the whirlwind could ever cohere, much less speak back. Impossible, but not inconceivable, and therein lies the anguish. We are forever driven to become conscious of a wholeness from which consciousness exiles us. It is an iron ring. Strange, then, how almost porous this passage is, how lightly wry, how it seems to float over—or maybe *through*—the oblivion and fatedness it conjures. You can almost feel, through these lines in which all life is lost, life streaming. I wish Bronk could have allowed this opening stanza to stand on its own (the poem as a whole, which tries to work through the argument, is turgid). I wish he'd allowed this elusive, allusive sparrow (Matthew 10:29) to ramify into the silence its existence has conjured, freed not only from meaning, which of course Bronk never claims for it, but from the *need* to mean.

v.

"Silence is not only the source of sound but its subject, and since the speaker's acquaintance with it is through himself, it is the speaker also."

"Nothing is worth saying, nothing is worth doing except as a foil for the waves of silence to break against."

"We live in reality without possession or occupation and the love of reality unpossessed transfigures us."*

---

* All three of these quotes come from *Vectors and Smoothable Curves: The Collected Essays of William Bronk*.

VI.

If there is a metaphor in Bronk—and they are rare—it is totalizing. That is, it's used to illustrate "the world" rather than any particular world you might experience with your senses.

> We cling like animal young to the flanks of the world
> to show our belonging; but to be at ease here
> in mastery, were to make too light of the world
> as if it were less than it is: the unmasterable.
>
> "In Contempt of Worldliness"

This may be a clue to what is unique in Bronk. The philosopher Richard Kearney writes that "the transformative and synthetic power of metaphor . . . turns contingency to essence." Kearney is arguing that certain artists not only manage to create such metaphors, but also that their art, for the reader, brings essence (back) into contingency—the word becomes flesh. This assumes some original connection between word and world, which Bronk is quick to repudiate. "We know nothing of the world and will never know," he writes in an essay called "Costume as Metaphor." "All we say is metaphor which asserts at once our unknowing and our need to state in some language what we don't know." But I'm not sure this is quite as conflicting as it seems. Kearney is talking about individual metaphors. Bronk is referring to "all we say"; that is, the totality of language is a single metaphor for what we can't express. He sought a poetry true to this vision of language and reality. The particular itself is not important to him, but particularity is. Oskar Fischinger once wrote to John Cage that "everything in the world has a spirit that is released by its sound." For Bronk, thinghood has such a spirit. This is why all of his poems have, in effect, one sound. It's like the frequency of Being.

VII.

It's no small thing to chisel an idiolect out of (or is it into?) the solid rock of one language. We think of language as being protean, plasmic, ever shifting and extending to accommodate a collective consciousness. And this is true. But for some poets a mother tongue is, besides this living instrument, a lumpen collectivity within which, it seems, they are trapped. One must somehow both inhabit that protean flow and break it open. This is a muddled image, I realize, so just imagine what it's like to live it.

A comparison might help. Whitman, so purposefully "democratic," so at ease with the demotic, invented a form, not an idiolect. ("An unrealized potentiality of form," Bronk complained in a letter, but never mind.) In his work one feels great tectonic shifts far below the surface of literature, not some violent crack in the magma. Dickinson—do I even need to finish this sentence?

"My poems come to me in their own language," Bronk said in an interview, "and if they were not in that language, they would not have any force." This is the dilemma of every poet (and it's a tiny minority) who is both forced into and freed by an idiolect. Basil Bunting and David Jones are such poets. Robert Frost and W. H. Auden are not. Gwendolyn Brooks, yes. Elizabeth Bishop, no. Bronk's place in this schema is obvious. His poems are quirks, freaks, almost belligerently unbeautiful, though that suggests a stance and not a nature. He's the armadillo of poetry: armored, elusive, prehistoric, a survivor.

VIII

"I deal with despair because I feel despair. Most people feel despair but they are not prepared to deal with it except pretend that it's not there. I think it's there metaphysically, that it is not a matter of an individual predicament. It's in the nature of reality and not to be denied."

"Reality is brought to mind by the inadequacy of any statement of it, the tension of that inadequacy, the direction and force of the statement."

"But the effort I want to make is not to become more lucid and straightforward but to become forceful and vivid enough that the discomfiting ambiguities of the poems will have to be swallowed and even a little digested."*

IX.

I've spent a month of mornings with the gray, flimsy Talisman edition of *Life Supports: New and Collected Poems*.† Somehow even the plainness of the book — it looks almost self-published — is heartening. And the way the poems are crammed together one after another as jagged and implacable as a pile of scrap metal. Nothing to see here, the book almost shouts. Or mumbles,

---

* In order: "A Conversation with William Bronk," *Credences*; *Vectors and Smoothable Curves*; quoted in *The Force of Desire: A Life of William Bronk*, by Lyman Gilmore.

† I also read through the posthumous collection *Bursts of Light: The Collected Later Poems*, but it seems to me to merely repeat, with diminished intensity, the achievements of the earlier work.

rather, as even his rare exclamation points can't lift Bronk's lines to a shout. Everything is bent, balked, Bronked. Many of the poems literally stutter. Lines repeat, break apart midsentence, backtrack—not as if stuttering were a deficiency to be overcome but almost as if stuttering were an aesthetic, as if anything said too plainly were a lie.

> Common sense is talking; it tells us what
> we have to believe is true, the obvious:
> we are born, we die, we perceive the shapes of things,
> and these are the shapes that anybody can see,
> granted good will, granted a will to be sane.
> Listen to it, oh listen to it. Yes!
> Hold hard to clarity. Stay here.
> But, Jesus, God, this is a world where we
> are under compulsion not to stay with the sane
> —where besides the shape of things, is shapelessness,
> randomed with atoms whose dance we please to be,
> all private, nothing and all in a world
> where the sense we commune together to make is wrong.

"The Duplicities of Sense"

All private. This is another essential ingredient of Bronk, a privacy so absolute that there can be no such thing as shared speech, or feeling, or "sense," or whatever. And yet this assertion is qualified as being both "nothing and all." And then there is that strange interjection, "But, Jesus, God." If he'd only said Jesus or God, it would sound like an ordinary secular curse, but the repetition makes it more intense and specific, as if it were an appeal, even a prayer. And it is a repetition: there is a theology implicit within it (and in the poem as a whole). Christ sacralizes matter and awakens (restores) a kinship with every human life therein. (Hopkins: "for Christ plays in ten thousand places, / Lovely in limbs, and lovely in eyes not his.") God is the comprehensive and comprehending "reality" before which every human understanding falls short. (Augustine: "If you think you have understood God, it is not God.") The sense we commune (another word with Christian echoes) to make together is "wrong," but the act of communing to make such sense has to mean *something*, right? Wrong:

> That we believe in nothing is a hard requirement because we want to believe in something: some political theorem, say, or religious creed or, sparing these, some unevaluated strength of our own as though in our person we might prevail and that prevalence had the salience of some proof. For what? For our dying? Because we do. Unable to think of ourselves this way, think instead of someone ten thousand years from us one way or another who will have or had a name, a place and costume no more and as much as we have. And who is he? Even so far as we know, it is a pretense of knowing. Abandon that.*

But to believe in nothing is a belief. It is a consolation to declare that you will never be consoled. Again and again Bronk finds (and suffers) the limit of what the human mind can know. This is a feat. But unlike some poets with whom he shares certain formal and philosophical orientations—Dickinson and Stevens, for

---

* *Vectors and Smoothable Curves: The Collected Essays of William Bronk*

instance—Bronk never discovers a way to release himself *into* unknowingness. This can be frustrating. One sometimes has the sense of a man lashed to a mast in his own living room.

And yet: *Randomed with atoms whose dance we please to be.* This is the kind of shining, autonomous line, and the kind of seducing music, Bronk usually avoids, and which therefore merits close attention. I'd read this poem several times before I realized I was unconsciously inserting an "ourselves" after "please," which is definitely one possible reading. But the grammar demands another one, which seems to me truer to the poem. Instead of ourselves, it's the purely material world that's pleased (which must not be purely material if we can "please" it?) by the fact of our being— provided, that is, that our being partakes of whatever kind of sense lies beyond that which is "common." What is common sense? "We are born, we die, we perceive the shapes of things." This different, saving kind of sense, then, must call into question each of these assertions. Perhaps we are not only born but created. Perhaps there is a kind of life that is not nullified by death. And perhaps we do not in fact rightly perceive reality until we perceive the excess existence brimming within it. I'm not saying Bronk is saying all this. I'm saying he's not-saying it. *Not-saying*, in fact, is Bronk's ultimate ambition, here and elsewhere. Not this, not this, not this, he says over and over, until, in the interstitial silences, some volatile possibility of *this-ness* begins to glow. "Apophasis" is the theological term for this. "Agnosticism" is what Bronk himself settles on late in his life. Both terms are a bit anodyne for the exhilaration and anguish any whole-souled effort at inhabiting this ontological space demands. Here are two poems placed right on top of each other in the collected poems, from a book called (remember that whirlwind?) *Finding Losses*:

THE LATE AGNOSTIC

Once, I thought I might once know
some minor thing of the world but a start though.
That was a long time. There isn't an I
or a world to know. There is something not known.

OLD HIM

If we are asked how we shall live in the world
it doesn't ask us. It lives us if it will
or else, no matter, leaves us alone. *Have
thine own way, Lord. Have thine own way.*

X.

For a long time I thought the loneliness of poetry was terrible, in
both senses of that word. It was a grief that every poet suffered in
order to be the voice that Being needed to acquire, and it was also
a source of spiritual power. Now I see that loneliness is general.
Poetry merely gives form to this fact and makes it available — and
therefore bearable.

XI.

Bearable?

I thought you were an anchor in the drift of the world;
but no: there isn't an anchor anywhere.
There isn't an anchor in the drift of the world. Oh no.
I thought you were. Oh no. The drift of the world.

This may be the saddest poem I know. As with other Bronk poems
it sends me reeling through my own life grasping after my own
anchors: my wife and my work, my God. Oh no.

And yet this minor poem brings me major peace. Why? Be-
cause it is beautiful, and beauty triggers an instinct for an order
beyond the one it enacts. And because usually we suffer the drift
of the world but do not really feel it. It happens to us but not in
us. One of the functions of art, says Kearney, is to make us active
rather than passive with regard to our memories and therefore our
futures, to help us move "from melancholy to mourning." True
enough, both in general and with regard to this one poem. And yet
every time I read this cosmically compressed elegy my chief feeling
is not grief or mourning, but *elation*.

How does this little poem accomplish all of this? Sound, form,
the frequency of Being. Much of Bronk's technical genius involves
repetition, careful substitution, deletion. The way this poem stut-
ters and repeats makes readers unconsciously anticipate, after the
opening phrase of the final line ("I thought you were."), that they
are going to hear the entire first line again. Which is what hap-
pens, in a way. The fragment (which can also be read, hauntingly,
as a complete sentence) disrupts the expectation, but in the space
occupied by the "Oh no" the mind, consciously or not, "hears"
what is missing: the anchor. Leaving it out, paradoxically, puts it
back in. Not-saying. In the middle of this ghostly poem there floats,

unaccountably, an iron anchor. Something of our deepest sadness, which is our deepest loneliness, has been faced and, precisely because it has been faced, lifted up. It is not in any way *lightened*. It is, literally, deadweight. Which makes the way it's been raised all the more miraculous.

XII.

Nothing left to read? "It is better to say 'I am suffering,'" writes Simone Weil, "than to say, 'This landscape is ugly.'"

XIII.

It is late morning and I have been sitting despairing over what a life in poetry amounts to and little three-year-old Greta has just come from next door bearing a book about the necessity for a second conversion that her father thought I'd want to read. She is curly-haired, her whole being golden, alert as a bird. We talk for a bit about the redemptive qualities of "asahgo" bagels, and then she skips back across the yard to her house. We are here, we are here. Set this down, too, as much as if an atrocity had happened and been seen. The earth is beautiful beyond all change.

READING PASCAL IN QUARANTINE

I love only those who seek with lamentation.
I love only those whose lives evince some timeless entire.
To weep is to see. To be is to bow.
I love only those who know a whole new naivete.

HOW MANY DAYS

How many days I wasted chasing God
when I could have been in bed with you.

I'm no gardener but twice I've tried
planting a little patch of something
back of the predictable.

How many days I spent spending life
down on my knees in that first dirt.
Little grew, and what did tasted vaguely of tar,
Tony's Auto Body, and fear.

How many cities, how much botch and rot,
how many seductions of sound and circumstance,
to reach, receive, as in a migraine a mite of peace:
It's not that of two truths you've chosen wrongly,
but that in choosing you've wronged it all.

I'm no gardener . . . but here I am, going at it again
in my aimless way of flinging seed,
where faith is the failure love demands,
and even the wrong sloth rots upward in time.

DROP A NOTCH THE SACRED SHIELD

A poem that's reducible to a message is not a good poem. A poem you can paraphrase in prose is not a good poem. I feel absurd saying such banalities, but much have I traveled in the Realms of Dull, wherein preachers and teachers and other professional talkers treat poems like wisdom machines or shortcuts to a conclusion. It's like holding up a river stone far from the river. Dry and drab, the stone gives no hint of the gleam that made one marvel in the first place.

So. Though I do love *what* this poem by Etheridge Knight is saying, and though it gives a jolt of hope to a part of my heart that sometimes seems hardened with despair, what I would first of all draw attention to is the strange, syncopated, joyful, inimitable music of its meaning. Ultimately the music *is* its meaning. I'll come back to that.

A WASP WOMAN VISITS A BLACK JUNKIE IN PRISON

After explanations and regulations, he
Walked warily in.
Black hair covered his chin, subscribing to
Villainous ideal.
"This can not be real," he thought, "this is a
Classical mistake;

This is a cake baked with embarrassing icing;
Somebody's got
Likely as not, a big fat tongue in cheek!
What have I to do
With a prim and proper-blooded lady?"
Christ in deed has risen
When a Junkie in prison visits with a Wasp woman.

"Hold your stupid face, man,
Learn a little grace, man; drop a notch the sacred shield.
She might have good reason,
Like: 'I was in prison and ye visited me not,' or—some such.
So sweep clear
Anachronistic fear, fight the fog,
And use no hot words."

After the seating
And the greeting, they fished for a denominator,
Common or uncommon;
And could only summon up the fact that both were human.
"Be at ease, man!
Try to please, man!—the lady is as lost as you:
'You got children, Ma'am?'" he said aloud.

The thrust broke the dam, and their lines wiggled in the
    water.
She offered no pills
To cure his many ills, no compact sermons, but small
And funny talk:
"My baby began to walk . . . simply cannot keep his room
    clean . . ."

Her chatter sparked no resurrection and truly
No shackles were shaken
But after she had taken her leave, he walked softly,
And for hours used no hot words.

Identity can be liberating and it can be oppressive. It can be liberating to discover and claim who you truly are. It can be oppressive to feel yourself trapped in identities that other people define. This is true for everyone, from Liberals to Christians, from ex-cons to cancer patients. This is one of Knight's reasons for foregrounding identity in the title. Nobody wants to be called a Wasp. Nobody wants to be called a Black Junkie. But these designations are hardly equal. This poem is incredibly generous in spirit—and it is *in spirit*: Knight imagined this event, which I actually find more moving than if it were "real." It seems harder to sit in a lonely cell dreaming such communion without the impress of an actual event to draw on. Behind this poem, though, lies a little prose poem that Knight also wrote about prison, where he spent eight years of his life for armed robbery.

REHABILITATION & TREATMENT IN THE PRISONS OF AMERICA

The Convict strolled into the prison administration building to get assistance and counseling for his personal problems. Inside the main door were several other doors proclaiming: Doctor, Lawyer, Teacher, Counselor, Therapist, etc. He chose the proper door, and was confronted with two more doors: Custody and Treatment. He chose Treatment, went in, and was confronted with two more doors: First Offender and Previous Offender. Again he chose the proper door and was confronted with two more doors: Adult and Juvenile. He was an adult, so he walked through that door and ran smack into two MORE doors: Democrat and Republican. He was democrat, so he rushed through that door and ran smack into two MORE doors: Black and White. He was Black, so he rushed—RAN—through that door—and fell nine stories to the street.

Here Knight goes to embrace his last, truest identity—which is the only one he was born with, the only one he could never change—and it destroys him. It's a trap set by others. A machinery of language and labels. A symptom of systemic disease, wherein even a Black man who has paid his dues and is actively seeking treatment and rehabilitation (Knight did eventually kick his heroin habit) is dropped back into the same absurd, humiliating, and often fatal half status that drove him to despair in the first place.

Jesus promises both the fulfillment and annihilation of identity. "You are in me deeper than I am in me," says Augustine wonderingly. "Therefore if any man be in Christ he is a new creature," says Paul. And in the Book of Revelation this whole world is both consumed and consummated by and with God's transfiguring love.

What I love about this Knight poem is just how modest its miracle is. No shackles are broken, no hearts are ripped open, no one has some transformative rapture. No, all that happens is one very troubled man in one very dark place goes an afternoon without saying "hot words." His chronic anger is eased out of a human connection, out of his own ability to reach out. Note that it's his question that gets their discussion going, his curiosity or desperate politeness that frees them, for a moment, from being only a Wasp and a Junkie.

Note, too, the texture of this truth. "After . . . the greeting, they fished for a denominator, / Common or uncommon; / And could only summon up the fact that both were human." "Denominator" suggests statistics and fractions; "summon" is shadowed by judgment and law; and all of these "common" sounds seem to be writhing toward the one word that, for both of these people, means freedom. This poem is so playful, musical, and buoyant that you can almost—but only almost—forget the abyss of bad circumstance, intractable misunderstandings, and hellish history that lie behind it. That's no miracle. It's something much more durable, available, *human*.

25

AFTER THE BALLET

I in my whistling instants
sauntering the drab concourses
or thoughtless under the plebian stars
make of myself a kind of company
that to its origin owes
only obedience to the one
injunction against despair.
O my lost dappers and sleeks,
my paragons of gunge
and scuttled luck,
all my fellow credibles,
all my little filths,
come back. Come back
from the sallowing past,
from the herd immunity
to miracles, for I have seen
a room of depilated marble
moving, a choreography of souls
that would have restored
my own even without
the demoiselle who,
in a moment so tensely silent
it seemed the soul's nerve,

swanned her arms, torqued
her immaculate back, and executed
an improvised, exquisite, and irrefutable
toot.

26

A BURNING WORLD

1.

You only love
when you love in vain.

Try another radio probe
when ten have failed,
take two hundred rabbits
when a hundred have died:
only this is science.

You ask the secret.
It has just one name:
again.

In the end
a dog carries in his jaws
his image in the water,
people rivet the new moon,
I love you.

Like caryatids
our lifted arms
hold up time's granite load

and defeated
we shall always win.

Miroslav Holub, "Ode to Joy," tr. by Ian Milner

II.

You only love / when you love in vain. I am drawn, like any "common reader," to poems that reach for succinct and universalizing statements like this. "Hope not being hope / until all ground for hope has / vanished" (Marianne Moore). "The end of art is peace" (Heaney). "We are what we are only in our last bastions" (me). Removed from the flesh of their poems, though, the statements become a bit bony and cold. They don't pierce or reverberate; they thud and nag. The end of *all* art is "peace"? Can we really have no understanding of hope or identity until those things have been crushed? Do we love truly only when we feel fully the ultimate futility of such love? Etc.

One reason modern poets became suspicious of abstract statements is that life is often inimical to them. "Love is all you need" works fine in a pop song, but in a marriage, or in a boat full of refugees, or in any work that seeks to speak to life as it is genuinely lived, it grates. "Go in fear of abstractions," thundered Ezra Pound, ironically but revealingly echoing the biblical injunction to go in fear of the Lord. There is severe contradiction between our need to speak of ultimate things and the immunity of those things from speech. There is also, sometimes, hope and rescue. "It may be, if you please, that contradiction is one of the signs that make us recognize that we are approaching the final truth, for it shows that man no longer feels the fear which ordinary criteria inspire in him" (Shestov). We only love when we love in vain.

Is the statement, then, "true"? It's the wrong question. Or at least needs different phrasing: Does the poem create a space in which the statement can be true? Still off. Does the poem create a space in which the question of truth is, in some sense, suspended; not timorously avoided but savingly evaded? Does truth move through the poem as light moves through an elegantly constructed mobile (a late Lee Bontecou, say), heightening and refining what it, at the same instant, lets go? And is the space only in the poem, or is it opened in a life as well?

Poetry is not simply "good at" creating spaces for this paradox (the speech that gives presence to that which will not be spoken); it can enact and enable the proper fear one feels when approaching any absolute (including, if need be, the absolute truth of contingency), and it can enact and enable its (the fear's) falling away. The faith that poetry engenders can be, for the poet, religious in terms of intensity and commitment, but it is, in my experience (both as poet and as witness to the lives of friends), both provisional and perishable. Poetic faith is a matter of nerve and instinct. Religious faith will likely emerge from the nerves (perhaps even from an experience in poetry) but requires a conscious leap. "One world more than our wounds have earned."

III.

There is a seed of horror buried in this sweet little Holub poem: those rabbits. As it happens, I have been reading about experiments on rats designed to find more effective treatments for human anxiety. Rats are "asked" to solve a problem first in normal circumstances and then after some trauma—holding them underwater, for instance. The result? Rats do not relish the sensation of drowning, it seems, and think better dry. Presumably those "hundred rabbits" killed for the sake of an experiment were also waterboarded, or had their paws relentlessly shocked, or their cages severely tilted to make falling feel both imminent and permanent. Is Holub, who was a scientist by profession, missing or minimizing the horror because of that? Or is "horror" an absurd word in this context, because who cares about a boatload full of fucking rabbits—as drunk teens in Texas we used to shoot them randomly from the back of pickup trucks and leave them where they lay— much less rats?

————

In upstate New York some thirty years ago a dairy cow delivered four calves and brought each to the barn when it was steady enough to walk. Each time the calf was immediately taken from her and, if female, either killed or raised to replace a cow in the herd, if male, placed in a crate so it couldn't move (no untender muscles), fed synthetic formula to keep it deliciously anemic, and, in four months, slaughtered and served as veal. Mama cow was spared these latter details, presumably, or at least her actions when she became pregnant for the fifth time (dairy cows are kept permanently pregnant) make any feeling soul desperate to believe that.

The fifth pregnancy turned out to be two. She delivered twins one night before anyone was expecting it and was thus alone. She took one calf to the woods and filled its belly and licked it to sleep under a tree. She took the other to the barn and waited there with it until the Great Takers came.

We only love when we love in vain? Eventually the owners did unravel the ruse, as every evening the mother came to the barn

140

inexplicably milkless. This is where the story ends, or rather, where it refuses to be a story. (The calf was male.) Still, there remains a lot to ponder in the cow's pondering of those two wet calves knobbling up for that first nuzzle at her teats. There is deliberation and initiative, action and consequence, memory and imagination. And where these things are, there is, inevitably—though its form may be eccentric or obscure, and though empathy is so easily and so often trumped by pleasure—suffering.

———

Recent evidence suggests that rats are capable of metacognition. That is, they can think about their own thinking; they know what they don't know. Imagine a test that grows progressively more difficult—distinguishing between duration of sounds, for instance. If you make it to the end of the test successfully, you receive a wonderful prize—a new house, say. But if at any point you realize that the test's difficulty is beginning to exceed your brain's capacity, you have the option of bailing out and receiving a lesser prize—a new car, say. A few humans are geniuses and will successfully complete the test without doubting themselves at any instant. A somewhat larger number will overestimate their abilities and end up with nothing. Most humans, though, will accurately recognize when they have reached their own limits and choose the car. Rats respond to different prizes, but respond they do, and in roughly the same proportions. For humans, metacognition is a prime example of what we call "consciousness." Does that mean rats are conscious? And if *rats* are conscious, for Christ's sake, then . . .

———

The first cancer drug I took was what is known as a chimeric agent and was made from a combination of human and mice molecules. I doubt the mice signed consent statements. Other drugs that have prolonged my life first burned out the eyes of rats and rabbits, ate through the insides of zebra fish and wriggly-nosed little guinea pigs. It never occurred to me until now to even wonder about these unwilling animals, much less to think of them suffering one by one by one. Now I feel . . . nothing. That is, I feel the nothing of not having felt.

      ———

As the crickets' soft autumn hum
Is to us
So are we to the trees
As are they
To the rocks and the hills

Gary Snyder, "Front Lines"

      ———

In his wonderful book *The Spell of the Sensuous*, David Abram, building on the work of Maurice Merleau-Ponty, argues that in all human discourse there is "a dimension of significance beyond the merely expressive power of the words." This dimension comes from humanity's original embeddedness in the natural world; comes, in part, *from* the sounds and silences of the natural world. To extricate human language from this matrix of meaning (by way of modern orthography, according to Abram) is to hold the world at a distance, to conceive of world *as* distance. Great things can come from this. Modern medicine, pretty much all of Western philosophy, history, and theology, endless bananas. But of course there are costs, and not simply the environmental ones that have become even more obvious in the thirty years since the publication of Abram's book. "For meaning . . . remains rooted in the sensory life of the body—it cannot be completely cut off from the soil of direct, perceptual experience without withering and dying."

———

Well they made up their minds to be everywhere because why
    not.
Everywhere was theirs because they thought so.

W. S. Merwin, "The Last Ones"

———

It requires no great prophetic power to recognize that we as a species, as a communal *soul*, have withered, and that as a direct consequence the world around us is dying. The despair is too much to turn one's attention to, so most of us turn away. If the entire sky is blotted out, why worry about the small smoke that keeps you, for the moment, warm? And art? What's the point of *that* at this late date? Either you don't really believe in the doom you so loudly and lamentingly deplore, or you have developed an impressively deplorable capacity for cognitive dissonance, or you really do believe we only love when we love in vain. A dear friend of mine whose work has come to nothing (publicly, that is) writes in a letter, "I remain loyal to the irrationality of it," which makes perfect piercing sense, because what else that most matters in life do we find and keep by way of reason? Love? God?

———

Then, too, I would argue that poetry is where human language retains, resuscitates, protects, and extends its natural origins. Poetry is both nerve and notion, instinct and abstraction. The tectonic volatilities and more-than-conscious calms of its soundscapes can reach way, way back—and powerfully, paradoxically forward—in both time and mind. Poetry makes nothing happen? Might as well say nature makes nothing happen.

———

metal, the ore in the mountain, exists,

darkness in mine shafts, milk not let down
from mothers' breasts, an ingrown dread where

whisperings exist, whisperings exist
the cells' oldest, fondest collusion

consider this market, consider this import
and export of fathers, half bullies
half tortured soldiers, consider

their barren last vanishing, metal
to metal, as the amount of unsown maize
grows and the water shortage grows

speak now of mildness, now of the mystery
of salt; speak now of mediation, of mankind, of
courage; tell me that the marble of banks
can be eaten; tell me that the moon is lovely,
that the extinct moa eats green melon,

that merriment exists, is thriving,
that moss animals and mackerel shoals exist, that
means of giving up, of descent, exist, and
physical portioning out, as in poems, of matchless
earthly goods, that pity exists

Inger Christensen, Alphabet, tr. by Susanna Nied

———

I have come a long way from the love I started out with—both in this odd little entry number twenty-six and in my life. Does it all hold together somehow? (A group of rats is called a *mischief*.) You only love when you love in vain, you only love when you love in vain. Say it enough times, with just the right balance of faith and futility, and some ghost of the truth the whole poem first enabled might make itself felt on your pulse. Do you feel set free? Me neither. "Keep your mind in hell," said Silouan the Athonite, "and despair not."

———

To train myself to find, in the midst of hell
what isn't hell.

The body, bald, cancerous, but still
beautiful enough to
imagine living the body
washing the body
replacing a loose front
porch step the body chewing
what it takes to keep a body
going—

this scene has a tune
a language I can read
this scene has a door
I cannot close I stand
within its wedge
I stand within its shield

Why write poetry in a burning world?
To train myself, in the midst of a burning world,
to offer poems of love to a burning world.

Katie Farris, "Why Write Love Poetry in a Burning World"

27

I REMEMBER YESTERDAY.
THE WORLD WAS SO YOUNG.

On the radio the scientist is speaking of other earths.
There are in light red shifts and blue shifts
and some people learn to read in these
the probability of planets that might harbor life—

Our life, perhaps? the fossil-voiced host suggests,
whose despair over what our species has wrought
is countered by wonderment that we—and in particular
   she—
might wrest from death a whole new world.

She is vivid and avid, this scientist, effably intelligent,
and despite myself what lizards into me
are multiple moons and dunes and other obvious
and no doubt inappropriate planetary metaphors
for a beautiful nude.

And God? the host asks shyly. Religion and all that?
(Who hung the moon and the stars,
I think, and changes deep darkness into morning.)
I want to kill it, she glees.
We've lost one world to illusions. That's enough.

Some people read the stars, some people read people,
some sit in a vise of silence trawling God.
Love and death, love and death, red shift, blue shift.

28

THE WHITE BUFFALO

I lived at a state mental institution once. At, not in. My father—almost, it seemed, as if he were attempting to externalize a madness that had been flickering in his own brain for decades—lurched from family medicine into psychiatry in his forties. First there was private practice, soon aborted. Then a stint at a flatland hellhole for all the blasted addicts and harmless, homeless maunderers of north Texas, where time ticked and stopped and ticked like a hidden cricket, and even the slow, heat-warped air seemed sedated. Ever inclined to boredom, ever upping the ante, he began traveling one day a week to the state hospital for the criminally insane, returning as becalmed and refreshed as if he'd been at a spa. He was at home there, my father, in that home for people whose souls are utterly, fatally homeless. It was no surprise that when a staff position opened up, he leapt at it, and no surprise the extent to which he vanished into that blessedly unprojected bedlam, all the time and attention he lavished upon his shackled, unmythical monsters. If the subject of retirement ever came up, he swore they'd have to carry him out on a stretcher. Which they did.

But that's not where I lived. I lived in an earlier circle of hell, where the most dramatic things that ever happened were the rare bobcat sightings that everyone, sane and not, seemed to have but me, and those sudden north Texas, earth-altering thunderstorms from which everyone on the hospital grounds, sane and not, ran like wraiths. That's not to say there weren't characters. Angela, for example, who was obese and bursting out of cowgirl clothes and screamed expletives at the sky like a rodeo Medea. Or Leon, who on his good days roared around the field between our house and the hospital with his arms spread out, and on his bad days walked from person to person asking if they had an extra flap, a functioning rudder, an uncracked aileron. (Leon was an airplane, you see.) Or Phyllis, who had bees in her bones, and was so winnowed, harrowed, and nearly transparent that it seemed the sunlight streamed right through her, and was so anguished and eaten alive with pain that some nights I could hear her moans.

Phyllis lived in the house, not the hospital. Phyllis was my father's wife, not a patient. Phyllis suffered from advanced bone cancer, not bees. The bees are of my own brain, you might say.

It was my job to watch over Phyllis during the days, to make sure she got something to eat and drink, that she could go out into the sunlight if she wanted, that she had not wet herself or otherwise compromised her dignity, that—in the long silences when the ticking cricket stopped—she was not dead. It was a small house with cheap carpet and a makeshift wheelchair ramp out front and a loaded .44 Magnum pistol on the bookshelf and prescription drugs piled high like plunder in every closet. I was a twenty-two-year-old boy with a badly plugged well of unfocused rage and a vague smear of self and literary ambitions that seemed to stand no chance in this tiny dry asylum existence to which I'd been reduced. I was there for two months, or maybe six. It all blurs together. I was punctual and careful, conscientious and solicitous. You could call that caretaking the most Christian act I ever performed, except that I was getting paid (by my father) and I did it without love, or with only an abstract, humanistic sort of love that would have made Christ—that avatar of, and antidote to, the horribly solitary and singular nature of ultimate human pain—turn away in disgust.

I was also—somehow this seems most distasteful of all to me now—taking notes. In my free moments I'd write down the things my father mentioned to me about the patients, or details of my own encounters with them, for they and I could wander around freely and at times interacted. (Once, in what had to be a breach of professional ethics, he even let me sit in on a group session. It was dull.) I'd try to reconstruct the word salads to which Phyllis, as the cancer advanced into her brain, was increasingly prone, and I'd note the red-winged blackbirds shrilling "dementedly" on the cattails near the lake, and the "spirit-like" sandhill crane so sensitive and elusive you became aware of it only as it disappeared.

Those notes, and the mind that needed them to hold this all-too-actual madness in place, eventually exploded into a four-hundred-page novel I wrote in a fevered year a decade later. It was about a loveless and godless photojournalist named Adam, who in his early thirties had returned to Texas and the state mental institution where he'd been raised, because his father—a man for whom facts were merely imagination's medium, a man whose absence/presence created acolytes and refugees in equal measure, a man whose firstborn could only be named "Adam"—had come home from work one day, sat down in a living room where there was cheap carpet and crappy furniture and a gun on the shelf, and shot himself in the head.

That was all on the first page—in the first paragraph, in fact. The rest of the novel consisted of Adam being drawn deeper and deeper into the world of the hospital, and his own past, and his own mind. His "guide," so to speak, was an enormous, mysterious patient named Tobias, who, Adam would slowly learn, had been very close to his father and seemed to know a great deal about Adam's childhood that Adam didn't. Intelligent, articulate, and sometimes violent, Tobias was neither sane nor insane, quite, but of some wonderfully but dangerously creative existence that made those designations inadequate. Endless identities emerged during the course of the book—Tobias had been a preacher and a judge, a murderer, a martyr—all of which were subsumed in the one he now claimed for himself: *I am that I am*. Everything in the novel built up to a confrontation between Adam and Tobias, between the first man and the last god, you might say, which I could feel all during that year like a strong gravitational force, and which I longed for and dreaded in equal measure. "I will give you the treasures of darkness," Tobias says, quoting the prophet Isaiah, the very first time that he and Adam meet. But he didn't.

It is a strange feeling to strand characters who have meant so much to you, to feel their existences at once stop and continue in some dimension into which you have no access, like the known universe expanding into "nothingness." No access is not quite right, I guess, since I have in my head some of what transpires between Adam and Tobias in that last chapter (Adam has to either kill him or love him—or maybe both), though I have never written it down, and now—because the thread is lost, the spark is snuffed out, two decades have intervened—never will. To compare the novelist to God is an old habit, but a better comparison is between a *failed* novelist and God, who seems conflicted about how—or whether—to finish us. And now I can almost hear Tobias's low chuckle as he savors the irony: that I, who in my novel could not believe in God, should, in a chastened essay of contrition or compensation or atonement twenty years too late, make myself into one.

Other characters, too, are still surviving—and still suffering—in me. Most are from the west Texas world of my childhood: laconic, plain-faithed people whose lives happened in gashes sewn shut with habit, and who—in that flat, cracked land, among its bristling cacti and thorn trees—seemed like animate instances of the landscape. There was Theta, Adam's mother, who, like my own mother, had Indian blood, and who, unlike my own mother, had died in mysterious circumstances when Adam was a small child. There was a "love interest" (I had, I should admit, a "money interest"): Quinn, who was also a doctor at the hospital, was smart, attractive, spiritually complicated, and perfect for Adam in every way but one, which he wouldn't learn until it was too late: she had slept with his father. There was a patient who thought he was an airplane, another who was obese and wore cowgirl clothes and screamed invective at the sky. Bouncing off all of these characters, binding them together and to Adam, was Nicky, his younger sister, who had been wild and wayward and who, though much better now, still lived in the embers of that extravagant personality. She was all warmth to Adam's ice, all earth and living instant to his distant, uncertain self.

Wishful thinking, that. My own sister, upon whom Nicky was closely modeled, has never emerged from the fires in which she lived, though now there are no fires, no embers, only ash. We speak of people whose "spirits" have died in them, but in my experience this is not accurate. A spirit whose natural expression is either denied or thwarted—at least in people who make you want to use a word like "spirit"—does not die but is transformed into a ravening abstraction that ghosts the person it once enlivened. That's my sister. At some point all the singular and vital energy that made a space around her in which you wanted to be, all that life and laughter seemed to stop at the edge of her skin, and then began eating inward. I remember sitting one Christmas in my mother's small apartment in Abilene, reading aloud the relevant passages from the Gospel of Luke that, at that moment, it would have been easier for me to eat, everyone feeling for their wallets and watches, everyone pretending that my sister, with her glassy jagged laughter and simultaneous cigarettes, her infested skin and fiending knees, was not using again.

This was after I had abandoned the novel but before it had, so to speak, abandoned me. (I still thought I'd finish it someday.) It was after I had fallen in love with the woman who is now my wife, but it was before I had fathered twin girls who bloom and scream in our days (and nights . . .) now like the earthiest incarnations of hope. It was after I had knelt down one day and assented to the faith that had long been latent within me, an ironclad resistance it would take my own diagnosis of cancer to finally crack open, but it was before I came to understand that the greatest danger to that faith would be not the dramatic crises of my life, and not the abyss of unbelief over which I am constantly suspended, but the endless succession of days in which nothing changes, no one ever changes. It was after my father showed up unexpectedly during the last hours of my wedding party in Washington, stumbling from guest to guest with a nimbus of affliction around him much larger and darker than the black hat he actually wore, but it was before my sister, with a child's tensed-lip determination that I can almost see, had carefully cut in half a Coke can, stuffed her mouth with an institutional towel, and dug one wrist down to the bone.

She was in prison then—serious prison, a two-year stint among some of the most hardened criminals in the state. At some point she began writing letters to me, though aside from those tense Christmases (and they were all the same), we had never really communicated at all since I'd left for college. The letters were earnest, God-haunted, well-written, disturbing, funny. I suspected it was that last quality that was keeping her alive in that place. It was suddenly easy to remember the person she had once been, easy to imagine her cracking jokes so brash, strange, and annealed with self-mockery that they could surprise violence into laughter. Other people's violence, that is.

One summer day when I was visiting Texas, before my sister had smuggled away that Coke can, my father and I made the five-hour drive down south to see her. Phyllis was long dead. His third wife had long ago left him and his fourth was, even at that moment, and though she was just slightly older than me, dying. I would have said my father was dying, too, as he was aphasic, and half-blind, and tottered about in some combination of early senescence, late-stage drug abuse, and the residual effects of blunt trauma to the brain.

He'd been attacked. The decline had begun several years earlier—come to think of it, my father's entire adult life seems to me a decline—but the physical debilitation, and then the avalanche into complete, ostracizing addiction, began in the midnineties. He had, unsurprisingly, migrated into one of the most difficult and dangerous positions in the hospital. His job was to "diagnose" the patients as they arrived, which meant, essentially, determining whether or not a given individual was sane; and since this was Texas, which leads the country in executions, and since in many instances these were men and women who had killed, often my father's diagnosis was a sentence of life or death. Protocol called for restraints and guards. Gradually my father got rid of the restraints, and then he got rid of the guards. He wanted to "get inside the heads" of people who, in more than one instance, had quite literally chopped other peoples' heads off.

There was one man—immense, intelligent, inscrutable—who fit into this last category. My father got to know the man, "befriended" him, I suppose, and learned not only of his predictably awful childhood and his appetite for intimate death, but also of his aspirations, his inner turmoils, his "demons." Thus it was a great surprise to the man when, at the hearing to determine his sanity, my father testified that the man was in fact quite sane, that he had known exactly what he was doing and should stand trial for the murders. A greater surprise, though, was in store for my father, who sat dumbfounded and enraged when the judge, who in most instances simply signs off on the conclusion of the psychiatrist, inexplicably decided that the man was out of his mind. There is only one hospital for the criminally insane in Texas. There was only one place for that man and his new purpose in life, his consuming and almost blissful sense of vengeance, to go.

Six months passed. The man was relegated to the remote and mostly sequestered screamrooms of the lifer ward, from which no one is ever released. One night after my father had worked fifteen hours straight, he was on his way home. There was a rule in the hospital that no one who worked there was ever left alone. The patients had some leeway to wander—they were, as my father said, "chemically restrained"—but still, attacks and fights were frequent, and there had to be another person present who could at the very least call for help. On this night, though, everyone was gone or dispersed, the wards were all locked down, and it seemed to my father foolish and even selfish to call a guard simply to walk him to his car. Foolish, too, not to take the shortcut through the dining hall, which was empty at this hour. He was already twenty feet into the dark room, anticipating his first bourbon and Vicodin cocktail, before he saw that wrathful and single-minded man sitting calmly in a little folding chair as if he'd been waiting there for six months, smiling as he stood with his arms extended as if for an embrace.

My father told the story entirely without bitterness, made it seem entirely his own fault that his jaw had been shattered like sandstone, one eye half gouged out, every rib cleanly broken with professional precision. There was almost a sense of excitement, in fact, or at least a kind of pained awe whenever he would set to wondering again at the devotion and calculation the man had shown, the coming together of chance and plan, the almost artistic ingenuity of it. And then—this best of all—to walk away, to take a life without taking a life, to kill only the spirit, to murder *metaphorically*.

The visit with my sister was two hours long. It felt like two months. My father and I quickly got in an argument over, of all things, global warming. (My sister seemed not to have heard of it, though she may have cannily feigned that.) Then there were some rote questions and answers about life in the prison, innocuous talk about my sister's two teenage sons. I remember my sister, who has smoked since she was fourteen and now suddenly couldn't, devouring candy bars and downing sodas as if all her manic intensity had homed in on sweets. I remember guards walking over once when a prisoner's hands disappeared from on top of the table, making her stand, patting her down. Mostly, though, even though the room was loud and we were speaking, I have the sense of silence—a vast and essentially lifelong silence—in which our various madnesses grappled like tarantulas on the table between us.

The end of the visit, though, had some bite. With about fifteen minutes left my sister asked me—suddenly, ingenuously—how I lived with death, what it was like to feel it so close to you all the time. I told her—hesitantly, disingenuously—that one gets used to it, that I had no symptoms at the moment and thus the disease was largely abstract. She asked me if I believed in God, and I said yes. She asked me if I believed that God would forgive anything, and I said I didn't really think about God like that, that I didn't think of him as an entity that judged and loved as we understand those terms. Whether she was confused by what I had said or saw it for the evasive sophistry that, in this context, it was, she merely paused. After a minute she said it was amazing how present Christ was in this place, how she could feel him here as she never had before; how sometimes from the very center of suffering—these are not her words, I forget her words, or maybe there were no words—there bloomed a seed of being. Not meaning. Being. A peace of and with being, and a peace that being, when the self it sparks is entirely ash, will not end.

My father took her hand. Then—dismissing me, it seemed—she asked if I would buy her one more piece of candy. I bought it, took it to the guard for him to unwrap (apparently at some point some very clever and determined criminal had figured out a way to fashion a weapon out of candy wrappers), and carried it back to the table. My sister's relationship with our father has always been even stranger—at once more intimate and more poisonous—than my own, and whatever kinship or abyss they had broached while I'd been gone sealed shut as I returned. My sister made a joke about how she was going to get fat (she was brittle and bony, her very self a cell), and my father shook his head laughingly and said how stupid they were at this prison, that they would insist on unwrapping the candy bars while allowing the prisoners to have cans of soda, which any fool could cut in half to cut a throat. My sister, chewing that last candy bar without relish, never even looked up.

Such drama. Such cinematic details. It's probably obvious why I might have wanted to write a novel out of this "milieu." Perhaps it's also apparent why such a project might be, for me at least, doomed. It's not that I was "too close to my material," to use the common—and often correct—workshop diagnosis. It's that I wasn't close enough, and my demand for distance, my fear of exploiting my subject—my fear *of* my subject—led me to impose an elaborate plot on material as uncertain and volatile as atoms, to move too freely, too confidently, through the dense and tenuous layers of memory, elasticizing facts, hypothesizing God.

What I want to say now—it will sound crazy—is that these people are not crazy. (*These people*—as if I weren't one of them.) They are not Faulknerian characters distilled to their most dire moments and neuroses. Or perhaps they are just not "characters," and that's the problem. I want it to be fiction, just as I often want God to be pure imagination, pure mystical abstraction, and not, for instance, the harrowing call of Christ in the dying eyes of someone I do not love. My family's story often *feels* like fiction to me, especially when I try—as I have been trying here—to tell it to other people. But then something happens, and I experience again the ruthless, relentless nature of its truth.

In 2009 I went home to take care of my father's affairs—just like Adam in my novel, I guess, though it never occurred to me at the time, probably because my father was not dead, at least not biologically. He and my sister—who had survived her suicide attempt, and survived the inexplicable (and inexplicably brutal) month in solitary confinement that followed—were living in a nondescript house in Fort Worth. Because of multiple instances of fraud, my father's accounts had been frozen, and because neither he nor my sister could figure out how to remedy this situation, they were screaming into a hell of withdrawal together. My sister called every day to tell me dully that our father was now naked and waving his hands in front of the television, that he had found the keys and taken the car and crashed one side into "something green," that the water was turned off and the dog was gone and "the State" was snooping around and goddammit she was about to bolt. I went home because I'm the one who gets called, because I'm the one who escaped, because I'm the one who, though always without any capacity to actually change things, at least won't fuck them up even further. I went because I always do.

My novel began with Adam in an airplane imagining the town of his childhood, which was the town of my childhood: hot flat streets and functional houses, a few scattered ranch-style approximations of opulence; the squat high school and the underground pool hall (rough intellectual equivalents); the square with its ring of dusty stores that fused failure and survival into a single aspect. Anchoring the square, or maybe crushing it, was the garish fake-marble courthouse in front of which stood the stone albino buffalo that had given Adam nightmares his entire life, and had given my novel its name. Sacred to Native Americans, the white buffalo is almost inconceivably rare (one in ten million), and it must have seemed to the town's founders, when one of them sighted, and then blasted, a single white life in a sea of brown, a brave thing to commemorate. I saw it when I was home. I sat for a long time outside of time and thought of the clear but inexplicable image that had first prompted me to write a novel, and I wondered whether it was because I could never figure out exactly what the image meant, or because I so desperately needed it to *mean*, that the novel, which is dead in me, wouldn't quite die. It is far west Texas. It is the middle of the night in an empty square, and there is a small boy standing quietly while his young mother, with a strange elation the child can't quite find a way to share, paints a stone albino buffalo bright red.

After eight abrading days in west Texas, where everyone had gathered at my mother's apartment; after tracking down accounts and the people who had been stealing from them; after talking to lawyers and doctors and angry debt collectors; after hiring a home health service to come in every day of the week and take care of my father because he refused to consider any sort of assisted living arrangement; after my sister had vanished; after I had first learned that I was going to be a father, on the phone in a room adjacent to the one in which my own father lay on the floor moaning that he wanted to die, someone please just help him die—I went into the living room and picked up my father from the floor and helped him into his half-wrecked car and drove east to that rented, random house where he knew no one.

It took him five minutes to stop crying, ten to start talking, though it was difficult to hear him over the wind blasting through the broken door. Finally I did hear him, though, and he was telling me—or maybe just telling the landscape—a story about a patient he had once "treated," a story I had heard long before and had in fact put in the mouth of my imaginary psychopath, my lost psychopomp, Tobias.

Once there was a place that was hell, or it was heaven, depending on whose eyes, whose heart, was seeing. Once there was a man who had no reason whatsoever to live, or had every reason, if you could only see collecting Saran Wrap from Jell-O salads, from Sunday brownies and the pale shallow little bowls of institutional green beans, as a reason. The man was small and quiet and had been in this place for so long that no one remembered what had first brought him there, nor did anyone know that the man's calling—and it was a calling—had become to collect Saran Wrap, for he pursued this passion as he did his life: furtively, hyperalertly, alone. Whether it was this self-sufficiency that accounted for the length of time it took for the man to complete his project, or whether he was working on some timetable that providence itself had laid down in his brain, it took a solid four years. Four years of squirreling away scraps of Saran Wrap; four years of secretly kneading those scraps at night into one ball, weighing its balance, testing its heft; four years until the dawn sun struck the hallway window at just the right angle or the guard's ring of keys clinked a known tune or a bird spoke with a human voice, and one morning when the cell door slid mechanically open the man walked out and bashed in the skull of the first person he saw.

"Can you believe that?" my father said when he finished the story, which did not differ from the version he had told me long before, and not in its essentials from the version that had made its way into my novel. ("I made up that place," Tobias says—or was going to say—to Adam in that last chapter. "I made up that man.") "My *God*," my father said, laughing quietly and muttering something to himself, while I stared straight ahead at the feints and taunts of heat rising off the road, and the land mashed flat all the way to the horizon, and the sky so empty that it had no end.

CODA

I need some kind of coda. Sometimes I think that's what my entire life with my father has been—a kind of coda. That the original work it follows never existed only enhances the effect.

Also, there was a miracle.

Twelve years have passed since I wrote the essay above, which has been simmering all this time in a desk drawer. It was scheduled early on to come out in a magazine, but I withdrew it because— well, I didn't really know why, actually. I knew only that something felt deeply wrong about it. Now I know.

My father died of an "acute polysubstance" overdose in 2015. At the time he was living in a residential motel so close to the freeway you could touch the hum of tires in the walls. My sister, a few years out of prison but once again a dead-eyed addict, shared the single room with him, their lives demarcated by fixes and (at his insistence) Fox News. My father was a Trump supporter the minute he descended the golden stairs.

Two months before my father died, responding to a sudden tug in my gut, I went to see them. I was changing planes at DFW Airport and spontaneously decided to add a day to my trip. I stayed (snobbishly, he let me know) at the nonresidential hotel across the highway. "Come into our parlor, my son," he said, gesturing expansively at the space between the television and the foot of one bed. There was in fact nowhere to sit apart from the beds, so that's what we did, almost knee to knee, my father and my sister competing to show me the motto some previous occupant had carefully calligraphied into the bed cover—"Fuck da money. Trust no one."—and all of us trying, and then failing, to keep from erupting into the old ironic laughter that implied intimacies long demolished.

We all pretended it was perfectly normal for them to be living in this diesel motel in this tumbleweed nowhere. We even spoke of them perhaps renting a place together in Fort Worth again because my father's state pension paid him $70,000 a year. Even given the illicit expenses, there was an element of willfulness to the rot and squalor.

And it was squalid. As far back as I remember, I can see my father coming home with refuse from humanity's underside. Games with some crucial piece missing, used exercise equipment that never got repaired, sections of fencing that remained stacked in the backyard for years. This was no different, only compressed. Belongings were piled everywhere. Dishes overflowed the sink. Food crammed every cabinet and the refrigerator, half of it rotten. There were multiple vats of some powder that promised to fulfill one's nutritional needs, along with an expensive blender that had clearly never been used. A couple of years later I would read Elizabeth Hardwick and be returned immediately to this room.

These people [that phrase again!], and some had been there for years, lived as if in a house recently burglarized, wires cut, their world vandalized, their memory a lament of peculiar losses. It was as if they had robbed themselves, and that gave a certain cheerfulness. Do not imagine that in the reduction to the rented room they received nothing in return. They got a lot, I tell you. They were lifted by insolence above their forgotten loans, their surly arrears, their misspent matrimonies, their many debts which seemed to fall with relief into the wastebaskets where they would be picked up by the night men.

I—the night man—took my father and sister out to Red Lobster that evening, where he had a hard time chewing the food and kept pulling out his dentures and cursing. My sister, also dentured, pulled her own out at one point and clacked them in my face to punctuate just how amusing she found me. We talked openly and almost entirely of drugs—the allure, the fidelity of them, the existential relief one feels to know this thing is there when you need it (unlike family, I did not say, unlike art or God), and the demonic ferocity of their claim. Serious drug withdrawal is, in my experience, worse than extreme chemotherapy, because you feel not only that your body is tearing apart but your soul as well. A single shudder passed through each of us, another simulacrum of shared life, shared grief.

We were almost finished with dinner when my sister asked me the same question she'd asked earlier in the prison, what it was like to live with death all the time, how one made it through one's days. The first time I'd been irritated, as I always am when someone brings up cancer when I'm not thinking about it. This time, though, I was shocked. Surely if anyone knew what it was like to live with death all the time, it was she. The suicide attempts (I have related only one), the hepatitis gnawing at her liver, the undifferentiated days enlivened and annihilated by mainlining little hits of death itself. I said no one lives with death all the time any more than one lives with God all the time. I said it goes away, that terror (that joy), when it isn't actually burning in your bones. I said some other useless shit. As with her question to me in the prison, I couldn't take in the fact that she was asking not out of curiosity but risking a real despair and an immediate need. Somewhere in the ruins of her life ("ash" is how I callously describe it above) there was a spark still burning—and seeking help.

My children were five when my father died, and never met him. That was of course intentional on my part and I have no regrets. He was, for the most part, a gentle man, but he attracted catastrophe in the way certain people attract lightning strikes; and like those people, every survival only increased the likelihood of another blast. By the time my children were on the scene, my father was sizzled.

Still, I wish they could know something of his charisma, his capacity for surprising kindnesses, his utter grudgelessness and deadpan humor. One day they will read of him here and be even more baffled than I was.

My sister, though, they know, and love, and this is why the essay above has sat for over a decade with an unacknowledged sin festering in it. And I do mean sin. Because it wasn't something wrong with the essay that kept me from publishing it, but something wrong with me, who had, in terms of my family and my relations to them, sunk into the form of despair that doesn't simply refuse hope but actively snuffs it out. I should have realized that a person who can find Christ in hell, as my sister did in that prison, who can see Christ working in hell and love this *even as that balm is withheld from her*, is not a person whose soul is dead. Why must I learn the same lessons over and over again? That both life and art atrophy if they are not communing with each other. That it means nothing to make a space for the miraculous in one's work if one can't recognize some true intrusion in one's life.

The moment my father died, my sister, whose addiction to drugs had defined and destroyed her entire adult life, stopped using. It was as if the instant she touched the one death we all share—and I mean this literally, because she was the one who found our father—all the lesser deaths lost their charge. Not that it was easy. She shouted and shook and vomited and moved through a solitude so black that her funeral clothes seemed a reprieve. For days she sat out on the porch of my mother's apartment clenching her knees as if parts of herself might fly off in a wind. But slowly, week by week, the talons that for decades had gripped her loosened, and her soul slipped free. And brightened.

"Hope [is not] hope / until all ground for hope has / vanished." "Hope is a condition of the soul, not a response to the circumstances in which you find yourself." "We live in memory, and our spiritual life is at bottom simply the effort of our memory to persist, to transform itself into hope, the effort of our past to transform itself into our future." "Keep your mind in hell, and despair not." Familiar quotations to me, all of these (in order: Marianne Moore, Seamus Heaney [paraphrasing Václav Havel], Miguel de Unamuno, Silouan the Athonite). I have used them in this book and others, have spoken them hundreds of times from podiums. I have so internalized them, in fact, that in more than one instance I have simply uttered them as my own. (Intelligence isn't intelligence until all intelligence has vanished.) They have all been deeply consoling and useful to me in jolting me out of my own despair—and apparently useless in freeing me from the static despair, or from my *perception* of a static despair, of my family. Could it have been otherwise? To some extent. Sometimes we want a despair to be ultimate because it absolves us of action. Sometimes we simply seek protection from pain that in the past has found us too exposed. I'm sure my detachment included both kinds of cowardice. And yet, for all the active attentiveness and readiness it requires, perhaps hope, in the end, is like joy, not willed but given. By God directly sometimes, as came to my sister when she touched my father's death and turned decisively toward life. By God indirectly sometimes, as has come to me as I have finally faced this essay and the sin that lay at the center of it: a willed death of hope in the face of a fragile but furious will to live.

Now more years have passed. Now my sister is a tender and eccentric aunt to my children and a loyal friend to my wife. Now I can see that the destroyed person who lay naked (another inexplicably brutal punishment) on her cell floor with her wrists bandaged is the same indefatigable soul who, in time, puts her ear to the vent to catch—and save—the fragments of voices and lives that come to her from the other cells. And the child who could not only spark adults to laughter but then fuel the blaze by imitating their laughs—this is the same morose and imploded woman who meets me in that dreary motel room the day after my father's death.

She is in early withdrawal, but I don't yet know that. I have come straight from the airport and have brought us sandwiches and two peaches which sit untouched because a woman from next door has skittered in behind me and is now picking up one random thing after another asking, "Are you going to keep this?" "You won't need this, will you?" and even "Your father told me I could have this."

I am too tired to be amused, much less polite. My sister is sulfuric with hate. One of us is about to be cruel.

Suddenly, all in one gesture, the woman grabs one of the peaches from the bed, takes an enormous bite, and drops it back down on the Fuck-da-money blanket, talking (now smacking) the entire time.

My sister and I both stare at the bitten peach. Then, at the same time, we lift our gaze to each other, and it's as if forty petrified years suddenly crack open in a jag of laughter so anarchic and original that even the crazy neighbor—still talking, and with apparently no inkling of its source—can't keep herself from joining in.

HOW TO LIVE

A grudge of clouds, little spats of rain,
afternoon an everywhere of seethe and haze
as of some malocclusion in the brain
until, *crash*, the downrush and whiplash
of the pent wind and the hellcat hail
shattering the glass of seventy-one Chevrolets.
Poor Mal, old pal, dead a decade now,
yet salt and sudden in your boots and gallons,
surveying this disastrous after
with nary a curse, nor hissy to pitch,
but calmly, wonderingly to lift
a lug of ice big as a pig's snout
and, like a token of unluck, and with that avalanching laugh,
crash it through the one windshield in your lot
miraculously unstruck.

BOMB

A Pit—but Heaven over it—
And Heaven beside, and Heaven abroad;
And yet a Pit—
With Heaven over it.

A Dickinson every ten clicks, it seems. There are worse ways to mark—and to suffer, and to treasure—time.

To stir would be to slip—
To look would be to drop—
To dream—to sap the Prop
That holds my chances up.
Ah! Pit! With Heaven over it!

I am tired of the word "despair." The drama that attaches to it detracts from the dull actuality that usually obtains, when one can't even read poetry, much less write it; one can't believe in life, much less God. And in those instances when it's not entirely dull? An electroconvulsive cold, an incandescent dark, still a pit, to be sure, and still quite annihilating—but the stun of heaven over it!

A wrong move is ruin. To avoid ("to stir"), to indulge ("to look")—wrong moves. Even imagination is perilous. "To dream" is to conjure an otherwhere, or another self to suffer, but in any event to evade both the scathe ("Ah! Pit!") and the ecstasy ("With Heaven over it!") of reality.

The depth is all my thought—

What this does not mean is that the depth is all *in* her thoughts. *Myself am hell* is a more adequate analogue and gloss. Or: "All my thought" is pinned to this pit. Or: Every pit is absolutely specific, as ineluctably ours as is our shadow. There is nowhere to go to be free of it. There is no one else to be.

> I dare not ask my feet—
> 'Twould start us where we sit
> So straight you'd scarce suspect
> It was a Pit—with fathoms under it
> It's Circuit just the same
> Whose Doom to whom
> 'Twould start them—

For "start" (first instance) read "startle." For "It's" read "Its." For "start" (second instance) read either "startle" or "initiate." Of the last three lines I might, if under duress, say something like, "The pit, which wrong action would have disguised, is in fact the same abyss that has devoured all those impatient others; we exist, no matter what, on tenterhooks in some primordial fear of falling." But the gloss is obnoxious. The point is to live in the lines without untangling either them or yourself.

"Spasmodic" is the word that Thomas Higginson, the editor of *The Atlantic Monthly* who famously took an interest in ED (as one would "take an interest" in a tornado), used to describe her poetry. True enough, though a deeper and more useful truth is that language, for Dickinson, is like matter for God: plasmic, primordial, always under great pressure, always some impossible fusion of miracle beauty and brute law.

Also, she made mistakes ("It's"!)*. Extreme isolation can deform as well as protect and develop a gift. Creation includes ticks as well as tigers.

One more thing: the "us" in the second line of this passage. Her and her feet? Absurd, but I suppose the reading can't be entirely avoided. There is often an element of dissociation to Dickinson, who feels funerals in her brain and buzzing flies after her death. We love her (insofar as one can love a tornado) because she wrests from her psychic splits and storms metaphors that clarify—and even make navigable—our own:

> There is a pain—so utter—
> It swallows substance up—
> Then covers the Abyss with Trance—
> So memory can step
> Around—across—upon it—
> As One within a Swoon—
> Goes safely—where an open eye—
> Would drop Him—Bone by Bone—

The "Swoon" here is vaguely analogous to the "dream" above, but this is a swoon of survival, not an escapist mist. Poetry can be a means of such survival. So can God. Both can also be escapist mists. How to move, then, from a trance to a clear awareness of

---

* Many editors and internet posters have corrected this contraction. But what Dickinson originally wrote was "It's."

what one faces and what resources one has to deal with that? From art to life, say? From rapture to ordinary reality? From despair (the old word, but honed by her, I hope) to calm? Here's how the pit poem ends:

> We—could tremble—
> But since we got a Bomb—
> And held it in our bosom—
> Nay—Hold it—it is calm—

Now who's the "we"? Pretty far from the listening feet, by this point, which in any event would have to have become prehensile. She could still be addressing a fractured self, though the hyperpolite "nay" is odd in that instance (in any instance?). Or it could be one of the thwarted loves our greed and weakness love to give her. ("Greed and weakness" because we want to bring her down to our level, as if our own abstentions and repressions ever brought forth such a flood of wonders.) Or is the "we" her and God? Her and her soul? Or her and us, her readers? Isn't this fun?

Here's a better solution:

With strong-willed imaginations it's vital to stress the gains that accompany the pains of denial and longing. During these extraordinary years the poet is distilling theorems of experience from her life: desire, parting, death-in-life, spiritual quickening, the creative charge and creative detachment just short of freezing. I want to propose that her poems work when a theorem is applied to a *reader's* life. It's a mistake to spot Dickinson in all her poems; the real challenge is to find our selves. She demands a reciprocal response, a complementary act of introspection. For the poem to work fully we have to complete it with our own thoughts and feelings. Her dash is not casual; it's a prompt, bringing the reader to the brink of words; there is the need to speak, if only to ourselves. This can be especially effective when we are in touch with feelings as intense as the poet's own: it might be abandonment or grief or fear of losing control. A Dickinson poem can open out into any number of dramas to fill its compelling spaces. As a woman unmodified by mating [!], a stranger to her time, speaking for those who are not members of the dominant group, Dickinson's dashes push the language apart to open up the space where we live without language.

Lyndall Gordon, *Lives Like Loaded Guns:*
Emily Dickinson and Her Family's Feuds

Each of us must ask ourselves who is the "we" when we are alone and in crisis. And what explosive thing is in our lives which, if "we" could learn to hold it well, might hold an even graver danger off? Or at bay. The poem implies an end to trembling, but the assurance is complicated, to put it mildly, by the image, and the not-quite-rhyme that keeps one, as the poem ends, not-quite-calm. *Navigable* storms, I said, not tame ones.

31

REMEMBERING A CITY AND A SICKNESS

Zapped rats abounded
on signs behind that house
but never once did we see one.
Zapped, that is.

We kept such watch as we could manage
in those days,
when such hurt kept us
alert to (it seemed)

vaster things:
Heaven, say, which remains
as remote a thought as pain
when pain is gone.

Where do they,
did they,
go,
the zapped rats, I mean,

which must have scorched
and must have screeched
and must have thudded
like hirsute breadfruit

down the darksome alleys
which every morning,
I'm here to tell you,
were clean.

Of rats, I mean.

Funny, as in strange,
that now, out of range
of rats and reason
to watch for them,

it's the signs that jolt
me back: an ecstatic rat
riding a red lightning bolt,
as if inspired to die.

How much of now's
a touch of never,
a gasp of vastness
like the end of was.

Funny, what I remember:
one dawn: two lit abysmal eyes
meeting mine
amid the prodigal rot.

Funny, as in not.

32

WRITING IN THE SAND

> They say unto him, Master, this woman was taken in adultery, in the very act. Now Moses in the law commanded us, that such should be stoned: but what sayest thou? . . . But Jesus stooped down, and with his finger wrote on the ground, as though he heard them not.
>
> **John 8:4–6**

A few years ago I gave the convocation address at Yale Divinity School, where I have now taught for a decade. Not only did I happen to be reading George Marsden's biography of the great eighteenth-century minister and theologian Jonathan Edwards, who was both a student and tutor at Yale during the years when its entire raison d'être was divinity, but I happened to have paused in the book at precisely the moment when Edwards himself was about to address the student body. Teaching in an institution to which I would not have been admitted as a student (bad grades, bad "life choices"), I was flattered by the association, and it occurred to me that many of the students in attendance might be as well. To be welcomed into a place with so much august history, so much intellectual curiosity and attainment, so many great names—surely it's worth a moment of pride. But maybe just a moment. In the last chapter of Marsden's book I came across a quote from Ezra Stiles, who was president of Yale when Edwards died. "In another genera- tion," said old Ezra, the works of Jonathan Edwards "will pass into as transient notice perhaps scarce above oblivion, and when posterity occasionally comes across them in the rubbish of libraries, the rare characters who may read and be pleased with them will be looked upon as singular and whimsical."

The pride of accomplishment, the humility of being you. The glory of the door, the reality of the room. These are ancient (and deeply entangled) themes.

There is a profound tension in the eighteenth century between divine grace and human reason. Grace is absolutely beyond all human capacity, one thinker after another (including Edwards) will say, and then they begin furiously reasoning their way toward it. The idolatry of logic—and it does often seem like this—led to some miraculous discoveries, like those of Isaac Newton. And it led to some pretty strange Nostradamus-like noodlings in the margins of the Book of Revelation as one thinker after another tried to pin down the exact instant of the Rapture. Newton himself engaged in this activity, as did Edwards. In preparing for that talk at Yale, in fact, Edwards read repeatedly the verse from Revelation 16 in which "there fell upon men a great hail out of heaven, every stone about the weight of a talent" and told himself that the hail, in this instance, would be his own remorseless rhetoric, which he would unleash (in Latin) upon any Antichrist (that is, Anglican) who happened to be in the audience.

I have no hailstones. I have no Latin and no answers. What I do have instead are two things. The first is a first-century Jew from Nazareth well-known for his oratorical skills but nevertheless, at a crucial moment in his ministry, remaining silent and writing in the dust. It's a strange moment—and one of my very favorite stories from the New Testament. I'll come back to it. The second thing is another form of writing in the sand, you might say, and it's actually three things. Here is the first:

THE PLACE WHERE WE ARE RIGHT

From the place where we are right
flowers will never grow
in the spring.

The place where we are right
is hard and trampled
like a yard.

But doubt and loves
dig up the world
like a mole, a plow.
And a whisper will be heard in the place
where the ruined
house once stood.

Yehuda Amichai

"A whisper will be heard in the place / where the ruined / house once stood." By which is meant, I think, that even though our human pride might wreak havoc upon our houses, there might, if we have the proper humility, arise a living whisper out of the ashes, something resuscitating and revitalizing, something close, perhaps, to a still, small voice.

The circles through which I move, even the religious ones, constitute a pretty "safe space" for this poem. It requires no great courage for me to celebrate its spirit of productive doubt. But I must admit, I do hear the skeletal chuckle of Jonathan Edwards in my own mind, whose ambition, after all, was to be "God's trumpet." And you can make an idolatry of doubt. You can become so comfortable with God's absence and distance that eventually your own unknowingness gives you a big fat apophatic hug. One could argue that when doubt becomes the path of least resistance it becomes the very thing that a faithful person must most resist. And resistance is often a matter of language.

BACKWARD MIRACLE

Every once in a while
we need a
backward miracle
that will strip language,
make it *hold* for
a minute: just the
vessel with the
wine in it—
a sacramental
refusal to multiply,
reclaiming the
single loaf
and the single
fish thereby.

Kay Ryan

Initially, it might seem that this poem falls more on the "doubt" side of the ledger than on the "faith" side. The great stumbling block for modern consciousness with regard to the Gospels are the miracle stories. Why should we believe that the laws of reality, which seem so implacably inflexible for us, were mysteriously suspended for a few years in first-century Palestine? Indeed, there has been during the past hundred years a whole theological movement to "demythologize" the Gospels. At its best, such thinking has helped to resacralize matter and restore primary importance to immediate existence (human and otherwise). This is obviously Jesus's intention throughout the Gospels, even when—actually, especially when—he is performing miracles. At times, though, demythologizing the Gospels has led faith to take refuge in neutered and confused clichés. How many sermons, how many blurbs on the backs of poetry books, praise the capacity for "discovering the extraordinary in the ordinary"? For a thought to become this common is no guarantee it's rotten, but one might want to give it a good sniff.

Ryan's poem raises this whole question while inverting the terms. The miraculous is so "common" (as in beneath us) that sometimes we need to be jolted back by and to the particular. Don't be too quick to transcend, her poem tells us. Being precedes meaning.

And yet, we need this backward miracle only "every once in a while." Why? Because if it can become too easy to transcend, it can also become too easy not to. One can become so disenchanted, so adapted to the "reality" of one's immediate senses and experience, that reality itself, which surely is stranger than our minds can circumscribe, becomes pinched, partial, even inert. (Attention *catalyzes* existence: "The eye with which I see God," says Meister Eckhart, "is the eye with which God sees me.") Ryan's poem, in essence, unsays itself: Don't be too quick to *eschew* transcendence. Don't be too sure that Being is not filled with meanings that are the task of one's life to discern.

Being and meaning. Two ways in which the mind relates to—or, in the case of the former, participates in, even fuses with—life. Christ and Jesus: two names that are the source and pattern for that way of relation. Christ is Being itself. Jesus is one specific meaning that Being acquired at one specific date in history (and forever after). And they—being and meaning, Christ and Jesus—are one thing.

Now consider the moment when Jesus writes in the sand in John 8. The Pharisees have come to him in the temple courts with a woman accused of adultery. They ask what they should do with her, given that Mosaic law demands her death. This is a trap. If he says stone her, then he's breaking Roman law. If he says don't stone her, then he's setting himself above Jewish law—either way, he's in trouble. Instead of answering, Jesus bends down and writes in the dust. When they persist—in outrage, one can safely assume, because think how irritating that would be—he utters his famous line, "Let him who is without sin cast the first stone." Then he bends down and writes in the dust again.

What does he write? That's the first place the mind goes, isn't it? It's certainly the direction a lot of sermons take, though some scholars question whether Jesus could write at all. I'm not equipped to weigh in on this with any authority, but if he couldn't write, what was he doing down there? Doodling? That seems ridiculous—and incompatible with the figure of Jesus presented everywhere else in the Gospels.

Let's say he could write for the sake of argument, then. What was he writing? Some say he was writing down the names of those self-righteous and accusatory Pharisees standing around him and the woman. Some say it was their sins. One can even find arguments that he was writing down specific verses from the Old Testament. There is some scriptural and historical evidence for the first two speculations at least, but I have to say that to this layperson all three seem about as likely—and as consistent with Jesus's character—as doodling. So how to read this passage, which by the way is probably not even part of the original Gospel, since one thing that scholars *do* agree on is that this anecdote of Jesus writing in the sand was added later.

This is a job for a poet. Or, more accurately, a job for those who know how to read poetry, because this scene operates as a kind of poem. It's meant to be experienced, not dissected or "filled in." It's suspended between the metaphorical and the literal, between myth and witness.

Consider the mythic elements. First, there's the act itself of writing in the dust surrounded by inquisitors. Who does that? Just try it the next time you find yourself in a heated meeting. Then too Jesus writes with his finger, not an implement of some kind. The Word inscribes the word upon reality itself—reenacting, I would argue, and perhaps salvaging, that original moment when the Word of God became the word of man. Also, it's metaphorically suggestive that Jesus writes on the earth, not on a tablet, as if the law had come alive, as if the closed world of human religion represented by the Pharisees had been blown open and shown to be as transient and perishable, but also as immediate and meaningful, as this glorious earth that is all around us.

On the other hand: consider the documentary details of the scene. We are told exactly how the crowd is arranged and the order in which the Pharisees depart. We know the woman is not simply being accused of adultery but has been "caught in the act." Then there's the fact that this act of writing in the dust really *does* feel like something the unlikely, unpredictable, and often decidedly unhuggable Jesus would do. It has the feel of a witnessed event, whether or not it was.

Marianne Moore famously described the successful poem as containing "imaginary gardens with real toads in them." The phrase is apt for this scene from John as well. It's one of those moments we come to again and again in the Gospels—whether it's a parable whose message is either implacably opaque or so transparently obvious that it amounts to its own kind of koan, or the silence after Pilate's question "What is truth?" which you can still hear two millennia later, or in this moment when Jesus "writes" something that you will never read, never "understand," and thus maybe, just maybe, never forget.

Does this mean that religion and poetry are essentially the same thing? Best to let a poem provide an "answer."

POETRY AND RELIGION

Religions are poems. They concert
our daylight and dreaming mind, our
emotions, instinct, breath and native gesture

into the only whole thinking: poetry.
Nothing's said till it's dreamed out in words
and nothing's true that figures in words only.

A poem, compared with an arrayed religion,
may be like a soldier's one short marriage night
to die and live by. But that is a small religion.

Full religion is the large poem in loving repetition;
like any poem, it must be inexhaustible and complete

with turns where we ask Now why did the poet do
    that?

You can't pray a lie, said Huckleberry Finn;
you can't poe one either. It is the same mirror:
mobile, glancing, we call it poetry,

fixed centrally, we call it religion,
and God is the poetry caught in any religion,
caught, not imprisoned. Caught as in a mirror

that he attracted, being in the world as poetry
is in the poem, a law against its closure.
There'll always be religion around while there is poetry

or a lack of it. Both are given, and intermittent,
as the action of those birds—crested pigeon, rosella parrot—
who fly with wings shut, then beating, and again shut.

Les Murray

God is the poetry caught in any religion, a law against its clo-
sure. God is in the world as poetry is in the poem, a law against its
closure. "Have you felt so proud to get at the meaning of poems,"
Walt Whitman famously asks in "Song of Myself," by which he
means, of course, that the very pride of understanding is just an-
other form of ignorance, and ignorance is not at all the same as a
fractious and catalyzing—as opposed to a cozy and complacent—
unknowingness. Have you felt so proud to know the meaning of
scripture, the right kind of theology, to know what you believe, or

even, perhaps, that you don't believe in anything at all? Perhaps you have forgotten the law against closure. By all means let us declare our faith, if we have any; let us be "God's trumpets." Because in that first Amichai poem it is not only "doubts" that dig up the yard and restore the ruined house, but "love" as well, and love is decidedly active and declares itself. But let us also keep in mind the ineluctable law against closure, the poetry of reality.

33

THE USES OF FICTION

I.

The mansion in Hollywood had a vast ballroom that was empty except for a thick rope that hung from the thirty-foot-high ceiling to the floor. The owner was a director, famous in that famished and downward way that the ascendant wolves can sniff out like weak meat, and the rope was, it turned out, his exercise. Every day he monkeyed up and down fifty times, or so he told me, and his barrel arms, baroque sexuality, and tenuous and strenuously tanned sanity made it an easy claim to believe. He was sleeping with my girlfriend's identical twin sister, and one night over sushi she and Sam spoke in their special language about the size of his penis. By that time I could pick up a word here and there. Sam lived in a ghetto compound owned by a painter known around the world for work influenced by "the deadpan irreverence of the Pop Art movement." It was rented exclusively to other artists, though the definition of that word was elastic enough to include a set designer and a bottom-drawer rock star. My favorite of the bunch was MacLean, a scotch-soaked Scottish painter whose outlandish life was inked all over his hard hairless body like cave paintings and cuneiform. Sitting out in the courtyard one evening after a young woman had delivered a litany of romantic sufferings, he said tenderly, "Ah, fuck it, lass, it's all just subject matter anyway." That was the same night that little bastard Harry bit me. Harry was Sam's disconcertingly percipient poodle, and there is a picture of me holding him that very night, something flagrant, almost obscene, in my youth and health. That was also the night we decided to destroy the baby in Sam's uterus, and the next morning I sat in the waiting room of a clinic in Santa Monica trying to pretend the decision had been difficult. One of the illusions of age is the feeling one has looking back at the past that there was a time before one's real self had emerged, or the wrong cells had begun to divide, or the moral sense had set like a foundation. "Necrotic," the nurse at the clinic said of the cells that had been removed, which felt to me like such a relief—such a *blessing*, really—that I couldn't understand the implacable sadness Sam assumed in the days after, the dark murk of absolute and involute silence she peered only partway out of like a lovely crocodile. Of course that is not altogether true. Of course we lasted only another month or so before I went back to San Francisco and the novel that would make me famous, she picked up with a director (not the rope-climber), I slouched into bed with a woman who danced in a cage at a club, and we drifted out of each other's orbits as lonely and inchoate souls tend to do. (Which is to say, not quite, as elusive and entangled as fog.) Years later I encountered Sam after a lecture I had given in a church in Washington, D.C. We both had children and exchanged pictures. The lecture was on the line between belief and unbelief, how there is no line, really, how to be devout means to be at risk, to live with the understanding that all one's assumptions might be overturned in the blink of an eye, that even the nothingness that swallows up every last atom of faith might be, if we have eyes and ears to perceive it, a piece of grace. The Greek word for repentance is *metanoia*, which means, rather than mere regret or remorse, something closer to a transformation of one's entire being. A certain static sorrow has entered the English. It will never come out.

II.

A butterfly is stuck to the mesh around the store-bought firewood outside the back door this morning. I watch my daughter watching it. Large black wings crimsoned with matching markings, pulsing like some exquisite viscera. It's appalling, sometimes, to see life pouring into a child like a torrent too big for its channel. Yesterday, coming out of the parents' meeting at the therapist's office, I said there was something about the nature of that therapeutic language that was inimical to my imagination, and D. said, "You mean inimical to your repressions?" A sudden squall, snow battering our faces like moths, traffic crawling down Whitney, another month, another meeting. "Tell me a time when you were bad, Daddy." Age increases experience even as it narrows one's possible reactions to it. Iron tracks have been laid down and long traveled. To deviate would require a crash. My own childhood was full of sourceless rages, solitudes so abysmal they retain exact position and proportion in the mind, like the objects left by astronauts on the moon that, because there is no atmosphere, exist exactly as they were. Not one particle has been lost or changed. But rage, too, is a reflex, I want to say, like grief, like God. There are times in one's life when form is a lapse of courage. "Love is the extremely difficult realization that something other than one's self is real." Sun-haired, sky-eyed, she turns her ten years toward the shadow that I am.

III.

His shadow lay over the rocks as he bent, ending. Why not endless till the farthest star? Darkly they are there behind this light, darkness shining in brightness, delta of Cassiopeia, worlds. Me sits there with his augur's rod of ash, in borrowed sandals, by day beside a livid sea, unbeheld, in violet night walking beneath a reign of uncouth stars. I throw this ended shadow from me, manshape ineluctable, call it back. Endless, would it be mine, form of my form? Who watches me here? Who ever anywhere will read these written words? Signs on a white field. Somewhere to someone in your flutiest voice. The good bishop of Cloyne took the veil of the temple out of his shovel hat: veil of space with coloured emblems hatched on its field. Hold hard. Coloured on a flat: yes, that's right. Flat I see, then think distance, near, far, flat I see, east, back. Ah, see now! Falls back suddenly, frozen in stereoscope. Click does the trick. You find my words dark. Darkness is in our souls, do you not think? Flutier. Our souls, shamewounded by our sins, cling to us yet more, a woman to her lover clinging, the more the more.

James Joyce, *Ulysses*

IV.

"Sin"? It's not a word with much resonance for me. Which is precisely the problem, my more pious friends might say. Pious, too, I toss off scoffingly. Once I wanted poetry to save me. From what? *For* what is the better question. To whom am I speaking? Tell me a time. They strap you down. They tie your feet together. They lock your head between cushioned clamps, for if you move then all the waiting, the fasting, the yearning to have an answer—it comes to nothing. Still I spasm. Every time. Can't keep from sleeping. MRIs, too, clang and bang and Katy bar the crazy, twitching talking up out of dreams as from sludgy water. Me to whom sleep so otherwise is, so warily comes. Kitty-kitty. "I just want one present for my birthday and well it's kind of a big one so don't say anything at all when I say 'It's a kitten!' Skipping liquidly off as if she were one. Tell me a time. In the noncanonical Acts of Peter, our eponymous apostle is crucified head down—symbolizing, some say, the inversion of values a life in Christ requires. Nailed, impaled, good Peter has the presence of mind for one last lecture. Scoffingly. I, too, am porcupined, elusive, evasive, rife with hate. "Darkness is in our souls, do you not think, Daddy?" The central nail between the beams of Peter's cross symbolized both repentance and conversion, the hydraulic drag of the past and the spirit's fling forward, the provocation of sorrow and the transformation to light. Two movements, fused. *Metanoia*. Though in fact as I recall the writer of the Acts of Peter sought to preserve a distinction between conversion (*epistrophe*) and repentance (*metanoia*). There are times in one's life when form is. "I don't really believe in God, Daddy." Love is the supremely difficult. Abysmal the stillness, the waiting, the end that isn't. "Only the man who has had to face despair is really convinced that he needs mercy." The butterfly wasn't stuck at all she says bursting in to where I am. It was clinging.

34

I LEARN FROM HER WHO LEARNS
FROM THE AIR

I learn from her who learns from the air
they whip pigs, the soul is curved and carved
like an antique table's leg,
Jesus prescribed menstruation stables,
and pets were once prized as wipes
for the feasters' grease.
For her a tiny pile of pebbles and shells
adheres as plover, then mother,
a chick *chick-chick-chicking* behind.
So many missed chances chanced again,
so many saving prompts and impromptu kitchen dances:
I'm a low hamburger, I'm a low hamburger,
pumpkin tub, pumpkin tub.
What did they know, what did they do,
how did they live with the lack of you,
when men were men and cats were napkins?

[35]

THIS I BELIEVE

One of the most difficult things to outgrow is the need for, the belief in, permanent things. Fixities, finalities, poles upon which you can place your hand and say, "This I believe," like that old Edward R. Murrow radio show from the fifties that asked great men (almost always men) to map their minds for us—that we might map our own.

> To me, mankind, a vast family of creatures, is growing inevitably towards a state of civilization.
>
> **George Leslie Stout**

> I believe that this hairless embryo with the aching oversized braincase and the opposable thumb—this animal barely up from the apes—will endure, will endure longer than his home planet, will spread out to the other planets—to the stars and beyond—carrying with him his honesty, his insatiable curiosity, his unlimited courage, and his noble essential decency.
>
> **Robert Heinlein**

> I believe that each of us finds greatest use and greatest satisfaction in a life which respects and kindles the spark of

the divine that is found in the conscience of every other member of the human brotherhood and which nourishes the harmonious growth of individual men and women.

Gilbert F. White

You get the idea. It's hard to imagine such confident encompassing sentiments now. (Indeed when the series was revived briefly in recent years it was striking just how different it was from the original, relying mostly on the modest observations and easily digestible personal anecdotes that are the currency of our own atomized time.) The sententious statements from the Murrow program aren't "untrue" exactly. They're not even wrong, as Peter Woit has said about string theory: the words don't contain enough meaning to meaningfully refute. Human intelligence and culture undoubtedly *have* developed over time, as these men predicted, but one of the ways that humans have developed, it turns out, has been an increasingly sophisticated understanding of the limitations of human development. The need for certainties, for "belief," is a symptom of intellectual adolescence, and it can afflict a culture as well as an individual consciousness. (And can express itself as militant atheism. And can recur. Cultures oscillate in and out of different forms of maturity. There is no straight line.) Religion often gets blamed for this addiction to absolutes, and rightly so, insofar as creeds calcify into mere concepts, are dead superstitions rather than the framework for living intuitions. But the religion that doesn't realize this, however lively and thriving it may seem in certain corners of the earth, is feeding on a corpse.

The one place in contemporary intellectual culture where you still find this language of human triumphalism is in science. Stephen Hawking famously declared philosophy (by which he meant all metaphysics) "dead" because it didn't—indeed couldn't—keep up with modern science. Brian Greene, though he is eloquent and inspiring on his own sense of wonder, believes adamantly that there is no such thing as free will, that even your decision whether or not to read my next sentence has been preordained by the anonymous bits of information in the sleek machine that whirs atop your neck. And these are the *physicists*, whose wispy theoretical musings sometimes seem akin to the intuitions of medieval mystics. Turn to neuroscience, where every other day there is some article explaining how seeing a police cruiser on the side of the highway causes your brain to "light up" because one of your ancestors was almost eaten by a saber-toothed tiger, or the cognitive scientists (Daniel Dennett: "The appreciation of meanings . . . is central to our vision of consciousness, but this conviction that *I*, on the inside, deal directly with meanings turns out to be something rather like a benign 'user-illusion'") and you begin to feel every last bit of intellectual and spiritual oxygen sucked out of existence. There has been some salutary resistance to this totalizing impulse (the physicist Marcelo Gleiser, for instance), but one would have to be in a monastery or a madhouse not to realize that austere versions of scientific materialism and determinism have permeated the intellectual air so thoroughly that it seems like . . . air.

As it happens, I actually *agree* with some of the assumptions made by some of the scientists who most irritate me. The difference is that I do believe they are assumptions, and I disagree with their conclusions. If you assert that we can predict the fundamental nature of human experience from the fundamental laws of physics, then you must admit the element of conjecture therein. Quantum mechanics doesn't somehow salvage the supernatural, but it does introduce quite a weird and seemingly ineradicable wiggle into the natural. More crucially, though, pointing out the physical nature of a metaphysical experience (the brain lighting up, for instance) says nothing about the reality of that experience, nor does a metaphysical experience, no matter how intense and transformative, preclude physical cause. Just as we do not seriously question the reality of physical existence—although we are determining that reality on mathematical calculations of elements that we cannot physically perceive—so we cannot discount the spiritual content of physical reality. "'Exist' may be too strong a verb," says Marcelo Gleiser of the electrons upon which so much of quantum physics is based, although no one has ever actually "seen" one. (Scientists measure their trace.) Well, as I have argued elsewhere,* if "exist" can be too strong a verb, then it can probably sometimes be too weak as well. *I am that I am.*

The idolatry of science that surrounds us now is a symptom of superstition and not, as the scientists argue, a remedy for it. The superstition involves math and matter rather than ghosts and gods, but the leap into belief, which is the refusal of faith, is the same. (By "faith" I mean an admission that our minds cannot know our selves or the universe in any ultimate sense; or, if one is inclined to hold—as many scientists are—that the universe and our place in it are knowable even if such knowledge is in its infancy, then an admission that this position is an act of faith and indistinguishable, in metaphysical terms, from a religious gesture.) Not long ago I sat listening to a brilliant chemist explain the immense existential relief he felt when he realized that every single thing about humans was explained by evolution, including not only our need to have things explained but our inability ever to fully understand those explanations at either the macro- or microscopic level. (Richard Dawkins has said much the same thing.) This is the ouroboros, the

---

* *He Held Radical Light: The Art of Faith, the Faith of Art*

snake with its tail in its mouth, the circular reasoning from which there is no escape. "No greater clarity should be sought than reality permits." Does it help at all that this quote comes from a renowned physicist? I expect not, for he—John Polkinghorne—is also a renowned believer. This I believe: that we—priests and penitents, geneticists and journalists, physicists and philosophers—all need to outgrow our need to say, "This I believe."

[36]

A SIGN IN THE VOID

I think the attempt to defend belief can unsettle it, in fact, because there is always an inadequacy in argument about ultimate things. We participate in Being without remainder. No breath, no thought, no wart or whisker, is not as sunk in Being as it could be. And yet no one can say what Being is.

Marilynne Robinson, Gilead

Faith becomes an instrument of perception rather than, as it should be, perception itself. It is a tool whereby modern intellects look at their lives rather than the living tissue of experience. Theology cannot help with this except to articulate the dilemma. Art can help, as long as it is always understood to be a means and not an end.

C. S. Lewis*

Doubt wisely; in strange way
To stand inquiring right, is not to stray;

---

* I have been unable to trace this quote to a particular Lewis book. Indeed, neither I nor my research assistant has been able to locate the quote, or any part of it, in any database available to us. Yet I remain convinced I read it in a book by C. S. Lewis. My notebooks tell me so. They also tell me that I will publish this book in 2020, and that Donald Trump will never be president, and that only neurotics and narcissists keep notebooks.

To sleep, or run wrong, is. On a huge hill,
Cragged and steep, Truth stands, and he that will
Reach her, about must and about must go,
And what the hill's suddenness resists, win so.

John Donne, "Satire III"

Since the eighteenth century, we have thought of reason
as a method: the application of logic to solving problems,
a steady, prosaic, and scientific process. To medieval and
early modern minds, reason was not method but a power of
perception: almost a sixth sense. For example: how do you
know that 1+1=2? Modern philosophy has struggled might-
ily with that question, but the pre-modern view is that the
question is unanswerable. You simply know intuitively that
it is so, and the (God-given) faculty of intuition which pro-
vides that knowledge is called *reason*. If you possess that
faculty, then 1+1=2 is self-evidently true. If your reason is
defective, or absent, you will not be able to see it; in which
case, there is no persuading you. Blaise Pascal . . . distin-
guished between the "mathematical" and the "intuitive"
mind. There are uncontested truths, he argued, which the
mathematical mind cannot prove, such as "knowledge of
first principles, like space, time, motion, number." To ac-
cept such truths is an act of reason, but not a process of
logical deduction. It is much more like a leap of faith.

Alec Ryrie, *Unbelievers: An Emotional History of Doubt*

I start from the conviction that many of the most important
things we know are things we know before we can speak

them; indeed, we know them—though with very little in the way of concepts to make them intelligible to us—even as children, and see them with the greatest immediacy when we look at them with the eyes of innocence. But, as they are hard to say, and as they are often so immediate to us that we cannot stand back from them objectively, we tend to put them out of mind as we grow older, and make ourselves oblivious to them, and try to silence the voice of knowledge that speaks within our own experiences of the world. Wisdom is the recovery of innocence at the far end of experience; it is the ability to see again what most of us have forgotten how to see, but now fortified by the ability to translate some of that vision into words, however inadequate. There is a point, that is to say, where reason and revelation are one and the same.

David Bentley Hart, *The Experience of God: Being, Consciousness, Bliss*

It was the last nostalgia: that he
Should understand.

Wallace Stevens, "Esthétique du Mal"

To cast off the idiot Questioner who is always questioning,
But never capable of answering, who sits with a sly grin
Silent plotting when to question like a thief in a cave:
Who publishes doubt & calls it knowledge: whose Science is
   Despair.

William Blake, *Milton*

The life of humans is nothing other than *a path to God*. I seek to reach this goal without theological proofs, methods and supports, i.e., to reach *God without God*. I must, as it were, eliminate God from out of my scientific life in order to pave the way for people who do not have, as you do, the certainty of faith through the church.

Edmund Husserl, Letter to Sister Adelgundis Jaegerschmid, O.S.B.

Where heresy does not flourish, theological studies are mere routine of office and constitute a way of killing time and giving occupation to spiritual sloth under the appearance of work.

Miguel de Unamuno, "On the Reading and
Interpretation of *Don Quixote*"

It is true that the unknown is the largest need of the intellect, though for it, no one thinks to thank God.

Emily Dickinson, *Letters*

How does a change in vocabulary save your life? Replacing one word with another word for the same thought—can this actually transform your feelings about things? Even after she stopped writing academic papers on phenomenology, [Edith] Stein continued to talk about the emptiness surrounding both objects and perceptions as being part of our experience of them. She suggested that emptiness—space—teaches us to mistrust the location of the "I" inside us, since it exists as a "zero point of orientation," being both at the source of the physical body and on its periphery where it, too, becomes empty. Space subsumes the structure of the person by waiting for it. Empty space precedes, succeeds, and accompanies our motions. But if all it is doing is absorbing and dissolving us in our approach, then we are beyond poverty in spirit. We live in dread because our body is unrecognizable in relation to a void that swallows the last location of the ego. The person actually knows the planet and the cosmos better than she knows her own self that disappears. She is unfamiliar to her own self. The Zohar—a collection of mystical interpretations of the Pentateuch—talks about this phenomenon, occurring when "the supreme Point and the World-to-come ascend" and where the end and the beginning become inseparable. The Zohar, however, calls this point Zero, the Supreme Will, or God.

Fanny Howe, *The Wedding Dress*

In the old Christendom everyone was a Christian and hardly anyone thought twice about it. But in the present age the survivor of theory and consumption becomes a wayfarer in the desert, like St. Anthony; which to say, open to signs.

Walker Percy, *Signposts in a Strange Land*

Every word is a doubt,
every silence another doubt.
However,
the intertwining of both
lets us breathe.

All sleeping is a sinking down,
all waking another sinking.
However,
the intertwining of both
lets us rise up again.

All life is a form of vanishing,
all death another form.
However,
the intertwining of both
lets us be a sign in the void.

Roberto Juarroz, "Eleventh.IV.45," tr. by Mary Crow

37

THE ROCK AND THE ROT
(A SERMON)

For a decade now I've been teaching at a divinity school. This is an odd place for me to end up, as I have no training in "divinity," if there even is such a thing (the training, I mean), and in fact I've never spent a day in graduate school in my life. A couple of years ago I preached at our commencement ceremonies and when I was sent a draft of the program to review in advance, I noticed that I was identified as professor of systematic theology. I thought about correcting it but then imagined the faces of my colleagues when they heard the title—some amused, some appalled—and decided to let it stand.

I'm a poet. To the bone, as it were. To the bitter end. Past every resistance, every attempt I have made through the years to shuck the mantle, which is invisible and unnoticeable to all but other poets, who walk around sniffing each other like despondent dogs. A few years ago, when my girls were just four or five, one of them asked me in an offhand way why I was a poet. I mumbled something about loving language and making meaning and was no doubt on the verge of explaining the extinction of personality when she grabbed my face between her two hands and like a tiny avenging angel, or perhaps like a miniature accountant calculating her inheritance, she said: "No, Daddy, *why*. I mean *why*?"

Many of my graduate students can also expect some version of this reaction. You read articles every day about the decline of the humanities and the job prospects for doctoral candidates. And ministers? Now there's a teat to attach yourself to, as my impecunious uncle used to say about our west Texas town's best oil-drilling company. "I hear you are entering the ministry," Frederick Buechner remembers a woman saying to him once. "Was it your own idea or were you poorly advised?" Pretty funny. Better, at any rate, than my despondent dogs sniffing each other's sonnets, though both are deployed for the same reason, defensiveness, social nicety, and both evaporate in the hard glare of the truth behind them.

> And the answer that she could not have heard even if I had given it was that it was not an idea at all, neither my own nor anyone else's. It was a lump in the throat. It was an itching in the feet. It was a stirring in the blood at the sound of rain. It was a sickening of the heart at the sight of misery. It was a clamoring of ghosts. It was a name which, when I wrote it out in a dream, I knew was a name worth dying for even if I was not brave enough to do the dying myself and could not even name the name for sure. Come unto me all ye who labor and are heavy laden, and I will give you a high and driving peace. I will condemn you to death.
>
> *The Alphabet of Grace*

Not so funny, all of a sudden, that calling. Not so easy to laugh away with retrospective wisdom, wry anecdotes, public speeches, sermons.

But what does that mean in the end—to have a calling? I'm sure you all know people who are so completely consumed with, and so completely defined by, one thing, that what they do and who they are seem inextricable. Think of an artist. "If you ask me what I am here to do in this world," said Émile Zola, "I will answer: I am here to live out loud." Think of an activist like Mother Teresa, who one day while looking out the window of a train felt something in the light and landscape tugging at something in the center of herself, and knew that she was being called to be, as she put it, "God's love in action among the poorest of the poor." Think of anyone called to speak the word of God. "If I say," the prophet Jeremiah writes, "'I will not mention him or speak any more his name,' there is in my heart as it were a burning fire shut up in my bones, and I am weary with holding it in, and I cannot." Implicit within all of these examples is a notion of something that is both inside and outside a person, some transformative energy that singles someone out, makes them different, meant for, and fit for, great things.

Surely there is something glorious and noble about being so chosen. And if you are young and passionate you may find yourself not simply admiring these examples but craving that kind of driven and meaningful life for yourself. There is something glorious and noble about this, too, to *want* to be so singled out, to want whatever lightning has struck such pure fire into these hearts. Maybe you're not so young, though. Maybe you know Wordsworth's lines, "We poets in our youth begin in gladness / But thereof in the end come despondency and madness," or that Jeremiah was mocked, jailed, and even thrown into a dirt pit like a wild animal. Maybe you have some idea of what it might be like to spend your entire life in the slums of Calcutta, and maybe you have even read some of Mother Teresa's letters in which, years after that touch of transforming love, she agonizes over the unbearable absence of God. Sitting beside a warm fire at night, sipping your tea while the cold wind whips outside, you might find yourself quietly thanking God that whatever that lightning is that exalts so highly, but costs so much, seems to have passed you by.

But it hasn't passed you by. You have been struck. Every single one of us in this room has been struck. To walk through these doors—even if it's only in curiosity, even if you sit in the back pew and pick apart every word the minister says, even if you have been coming into churches so long it's nothing but habit—to find yourself sitting in this place in the twenty-first century is to admit an insufficiency, an incompletion, at the center of your being. The church has remedies for this insufficiency, but it is by no means a permanent cure. That feeling of incompletion, that existential anxiety, that "tooth that nibbles at the soul," as that most faithful of atheists Emily Dickinson called it—I think if we are honest with ourselves we have to admit that this never quite goes away. You go to church and say your prayers and still something tugs at you all the time, will not let you rest *in* time, seems always to cast your mind forward with worry or backward with regret, to want something—to *demand* something—from you. Or maybe you drift away from church, away from prayer, and lose yourself in work or love, and maybe you're genuinely happy, you like your job, you're in a good relationship, and still sometimes it's as if you slide out of yourself and are watching yourself enjoying your life, or the words of a poem or song trigger some old restlessness you thought you'd left behind. That tooth nibbling at your soul.

This restlessness, this void that you can never quite fill, this tooth that will not stop nibbling at your soul—I would suggest today that this is the call of God. It is very private, a matter between you and God. It may come occasionally or it may seem part of the very air you breathe; it may come as frazzling anxiety or it may come as a still, small voice; but its warrant of authenticity is that it will not leave you alone, will not stop asking you: Who *are* you, really?

One of the most troubling moments in the New Testament is

when this moment of existential agony, this crisis of consciousness and individual identity, seems to occur both to and through Jesus. He has been praying alone—a crucial detail—and it's as if he just looks up all of a sudden and asks the disciples, Who do people say that I am? The question is general, social, a finger on the pulse of the people, "the blab of the pave," as Walt Whitman put it. You get the sense—I get the sense—Jesus doesn't really care. He was probably looking up at the sky.

Then comes the turn of the screw: But what about you? Who do *you* say that I am? This is much sharper and more specific. You can imagine it cutting poor Peter to the quick. You can almost see Christ—for that's who he suddenly and searingly is—lowering his dark eyes to Peter's. Or if you call yourself a Christian, or if you call yourself an atheist, feel those eyes finding that soft rot of doubt at the center of yourself. Who do *you* say that I am?

When I was a child growing up in the charismatic and claustrophobic atmosphere of west Texas, this crisis of consciousness, this one moment of existential decision, had a tremendous and eternal urgency. Into even the darkest hearts, it was believed, Christ turned those eyes and asked that question. Into even the darkest hearts, there came a chance—maybe just one chance—at everlasting light.

The tough thing, though, was that it didn't exactly matter what came out of your mouth. It was a closed universe, that town, and everyone said exactly what Peter did—"You are the Christ"—whether or not they believed it *in their hearts*.

So that's where the preacher probed on Sundays, saying it was a question that every one of us had to answer for ourselves, or not even for ourselves, since we could deceive ourselves, but for God—who, it seemed, turned his searchlight most intensely upon those whose imaginations far outstripped their experience. Little children, for instance. Night after night I lay on the knife-edge between heaven and hell while the question grew so savage and demanding and relentless that it wasn't a question at all: *Who do you say that I am!*

In all three of the synoptic Gospels, Peter answers immediately. In all three of the synoptic Gospels (and also in John, where this question does not appear), Peter ends up denying not only that he is a follower of Jesus, but even that he knows the man at all. The strange thing—and maybe the saving thing—is that Jesus himself has predicted this.

In the tradition of biblical literalism in which I grew up, there was one sin so egregious, so hell-foul and final, that even God himself could not forgive it. You could not blaspheme the Holy Ghost, as we called the *pneuma*. ("Slander" was actually the word our preacher used, which is also in the text.) Worse than premarital sex, worse than murder, worse, apparently, than engineering the Holocaust—there was this one betrayal, which might be entirely private.

Of course telling this to a child is like the old game where you tell him, "Don't think of a polar bear," and I still remember—still viscerally feel—lying in bed trying with all my might not to "slander" the Holy Ghost until finally my tongue was touched with an altogether unholy fire: "Fuck the Holy Ghost!" I whispered into my Tarzan sheets, bracing myself for the lightning strike.

The Holy Ghost, of course, is the spirit of Christ left behind for humans after Jesus ascends to heaven. The worst has happened: God is dead. The best has happened: He is risen. But now, because of some theological logic that theologians are still wrestling with, Christ must ascend to heaven and leave us limping once more toward what feels, for everyone at some point in their lives, suspiciously similar to oblivion. Our consolation prize is the Holy

Ghost, which is Jesus's presence in our hearts, which is sometimes damnably inadequate. Who do you say that I am? A ghost.

When my great-grandmother died at the age of ninety-six, I was twenty-three years old and living at the outskirts of Prague. I went for a long walk in a forested area near my apartment trying to feel something appropriate to the occasion. I spent a lot of time back then doing that. Trying to feel, I mean.

Everything was white: the birch trees, the fog, the sky, my mind. I thought of the way my great-grandmother's entire family had been wiped out by the flu epidemic, she alone somehow untouched. I thought of her being married away at fourteen and hiding under the bed from her hatchet-faced husband. I thought of her making her aching way to the back door and saying, "I guess the good Lord don't give us more than we can bear," which was the very opposite of the writer I was then obsessed with, Simone Weil, who wrote that "every second brings some being closer to something which he will not be able to bear." I thought of my great-grandmother dying with her stomach so distended by cancer that it seemed a grotesque pregnancy—all these things were swirling in my mind, when suddenly a branch right above me turned into a huge albino bird that I could not identify.

It was the closest thing to a vision that I have ever had, and I wanted—I needed—to know what that bird was. But every time I neared, it took off again into the whiteness, until finally, with huge otherworldly wings, it cleared the last line of trees and ghosted the mist over the river, escaping any name I might have given it.

Who do you say that I am? The power of the word of God comes not from its solidity, not from its being hammered into stones with which to beat the heads of humans. No, the power of the word of God, just like the power of poetry, comes precisely from its mercurial meanings, its tendency to slide free of every attempt to pin it down and to insinuate itself into every single life in a different way.

My great-grandmother read the Bible through every year of her adult life. It was, so far as I know, the only book she ever read. Out of the mouth of God, filtered through Hebrew and Aramaic, Greek and Latin, forged by wars and committees and blood feuds so fierce that even monks became butchers over the question of Jesus's divinity—down and down and down into a tiny little trailer in west Texas, there trickled the King's English ("But whom say ye that I am") for one old woman with no education whatsoever to ponder and puzzle and worketh out her own salvation in fear and trembling. There is something absurd and hopeless about such an effort, to be sure. And heroic. Forget the theologians and the scholars, forget the preachers and the poets: Who do you, Mamie Thrailkill, in your heart of hearts, say that I am?

How much of life is living up to a call we're never quite sure we heard? Peter's answer is the one that scripture has him giving immediately—"You are the Christ"—and it is *also* his adamant denial of Jesus in Jerusalem. It is the church founded on Peter's name, and it is the immutable muteness that lies within every authoritative statement that every church attempts to make. The truth and the lie. The rock and the rot. There is no one answer to Jesus's question, and yet you must wager everything upon it.

38

JOY! HELP! JOY! HELP!

Come, drunks and drug-takers; come, perverts unnerved!
Receive the laurel, given, though late, on merit; to whom
  and wherever deserved.

Parochial punks, trimmers, nice people, joiners true-blue,
Get the hell out of the way of the laurel. It is deathless
  And it isn't for you.

Louise Bogan, "Several Voices Out of a Cloud"

When the King of Siam disliked a courtier,
he gave him a beautiful white elephant.
The miracle beast deserved such ritual
that to care for him properly meant ruin.
Yet to care for him improperly was worse.
It appears the gift could not be refused.

Jack Gilbert, "In Dispraise of Poetry"

Too stern an intellectual emphasis upon this quality or that
  detracts from one's enjoyment.
It must not wish to disarm anything; nor may the approved
  triumph easily be honored—
that which is great because something else is small.

It comes to this: of whatever sort it is,
it must be "lit with piercing glances into the life of things";
it must acknowledge the spiritual forces which have made it.

Marianne Moore, "When I Buy Pictures"

White meteorite, infinity's orphan, word
Painwaking particular earth . . .

Supplicants, tyrants, it doesn't matter.
It *is* matter: unbudgeable, unjudgeable, itself.

Osip Mandelstam, "The Poem," tr. by Christian Wiman

We say: he has no talent, only tone. But tone is precisely
what cannot be invented—we're born with it. Tone is an
inherited grace, the privilege some of us have of making
our organic pulsations felt—tone is more than talent, it is
its essence.

E. M. Cioran, *The Trouble with Being Born*,
tr. by Richard Howard

I've done my best to immortalize what I failed to keep.

Joseph Brodsky, *A Part of Speech*

It is not so much what you sang, as that you kept alive, in so
many of our ancestors, the *notion of song*.

Alice Walker, "In Search of Our Mothers' Gardens"

I would like to write as if I had remained silent.

Janos Pilinszky, *Selected Poems*, tr. by Ted Hughes

I will write songs against you,
enemies of my people; I will pelt you
with the winged seeds of the dandelion;
I will marshal against you
the fireflies of the dusk.

Charles Reznikoff, "I Will Write Songs Against You"

Those who read or hear a poem should remember that a good poem has two audiences; it is addressed to the living and the dead at the same time. If a poet dismisses the living he becomes morbid. If he dismisses the dead he ceases to be a prophet.

Vernon Watkins, "The Poet's Voice"

Les Murray has said that rhyme functions with the symmetry of logic. The terrifying truth is that form *substitutes* for logic. This is the poet's unique power, to address the passions in their own language, the very power that got us barred from the Republic.

Michael Donaghy, *The Shape of the Dance*

Somehow she had retrieved from darkness the miracle of pure style.

Elizabeth Hardwick, *Sleepless Nights*

Land of visions and yearning,
This Mihyar is your barbaric saint—
He wears my lips and bears my brow
Against this age of insignificance that constrains the
    wanderers.

This Mihyar is your barbaric saint—
There's a god beneath his nails, and blood.
He is the forlorn creator;
He loves those who saw him and lost their way.

Adonis, "The Barbaric Saint,"

tr. by Kareem James Abu-Zeid and Ivan S. Eubanks

Poetry is primarily oral utterance, and the end of a poem belongs in somebody's ears rather than their eyes.

Etheridge Knight, "On the Oral Nature of Poetry"

Reading in silence is the source of half the misconceptions that have caused the public to distrust poetry. Without the sound, the reader looks at the lines as he looks at prose, seeking a meaning. Prose exists to convey meaning, and no meaning such as prose conveys can be expressed as well in poetry. That is not poetry's business.

Basil Bunting, "The Poet's Point of View"

The essence of prose is to perish—that is, to be understood.

Theodore Roethke, *Straw for the Fire*

The sound of a verse is the harbinger of the truth contained therein.

George MacDonald, *England's Antiphon*

But poetry cannot be an ark to help us survive the flood. It has to be our daily bread, an article of primary need.

Zbigniew Herbert, *Collected Prose*, tr. by Alissa Valles

An absence of spirit makes the writing greedy.

Tomas Tranströmer, "Elegy," tr. by Robin Fulton

I suppose you just gape and let your gaspings
Rip in and out through your voicebox
                                            O lark

And sing inwards as well as outwards
Like a breaker of ocean milling the shingle
                                            O lark

O song, incomprehensibly both ways—
Joy! Help! Joy! Help!
                    O lark

Ted Hughes, "Skylarks"

What is a poet? An unhappy person who conceals profound anguish in his heart but whose lips are so formed that as sighs and cries pass over them they sound like beautiful music.

Søren Kierkegaard, *Either/Or*

I am a happy man . . . and nearly all the poems I write are in fact praising things.

Norman MacCaig, *Twelve Modern Scottish Poets*

And he,
crafty, voracious, sensual, the supreme innocent,
between Yes and No, desire and repentance,
completely poised, like a balance in the hand of God,
while the light from the window behind his head
sets on him a crown of forgiveness and sanctity.
"If poetry is not absolution," — he whispered to himself —
"then we can expect pity from nowhere else."

Yannis Ritsos, "The Poet's Place," tr. by Paul Merchant

Poetry is a satisfying of the desire for resemblance. As the mere satisfying of a desire, it is pleasurable. But . . . its singularity is that in the act of satisfying the desire for resemblance it touches the sense of reality, it enhances the sense of reality, heightens it, intensifies it . . . makes it brilliant. When the similarity is between things of adequate dignity, the resemblance may be said to transfigure or to sublimate them. Take, for example, the resemblance between reality and any projection of it in belief or in metaphor. What is

217

it that these two have in common? Is not the glory of the idea of any future state a relation between a present and a future glory? The brilliance of earth is the brilliance of every paradise.

Wallace Stevens, *The Necessary Angel*

not so much looking for the shape
as being available
to any shape that may be
summoning itself
through me
from the self not mine but ours.

A. R. Ammons, "Poetics"

THE WEAKNESS MEANING TIME

All morning gently swimming
in the misery of a dead writer.
Poverty like a genetic bequest, polar loneliness.
The finical, fanatical, reciprocal chiseling of mind and matter.
And the long silences, late saliences of God and sound
set like glyphs in the mother country,
childhood. All morning, as if it didn't touch me,
as indeed it doesn't, mostly,
one daughter dead, another mad as jacks,
drafts and diaries scattered like a plane crash in the ocean.
Fragments as fruition, exile like a birthright,
and, as the sun bleeds out one evening like a suicide,
suicide. All morning my exercise
to keep these muscles strong enough to recognize
the weakness meaning time,
to climb out as if there were an out,
to dry off as if there were a dry,
to look back at a body of water, which, like all water,
leaves no trace.

BONE BY BONE

—*No* trace?

—I once heard a poet say that she couldn't teach Keats's last odes without breaking into tears. I felt embarrassed for her. Still do. It's not about being "manly" or somehow holding one's feelings in check while experiencing art. It's about letting art be art and not a release valve for emotional confusions or impasses—or, in the case of Keats, sentimentalities imported from biography—we bring to it.

—Excuse me, that's ridiculous. We're supposed to pretend we don't know what happened to Keats while reading his great last poems? Art is never consoling or therapeutic?

—I am often brought to the realization that literature doesn't pierce me in the way people claim for it. I read about a life of great suffering and go have some tea and toast and romp with my dog for a bit. I'm not saying art has no power. I'm saying *this is its power*. To distill the essence of emotion to a solution at once so intimate and so other it can't be cried over. It leaves no trace on us. And we leave no trace on it.

—What's the point, then? Of reading anything at all, never mind of writing?

—To keep Being strong in us. To keep us strong enough for Being. To memorize "the weakness meaning time," our mortality, our solidarity with other mortals, no small part of which inheres in our mutual understanding that we are, for all our connectedness and need for each other, ineluctably alone.

—That sounds like a trace being left.

—Maybe it's that I love language, not literature; consciousness, not content. Maybe it's not that they can't be cried over, these achievements, but that they *needn't* be cried over. Anyway, I'm tired of all this talk of literature as moral agent, beauty cultivating empathy (please), poetry as prayer, the endless instrumentalization of art.

—Seems a little late in the book to be declaring that. Anna Kamieńska and Carol Ann Duffy as teachers of prayer, Etheridge Knight as a model of momentary racial rapprochement, Wallace Stevens and Gwendolyn Brooks as shockers of consciousness (clearly a spiritual and moral awakening, as you have presented it), Adélia Prado as understated modern prophet. Etc. Why in the world at this stage of your life would you want to curtail the powers of poetry, which by the way are far greater than what you have conveyed in this book. You know as well as I do that it's not so much that poetry is a form of art as that art is a form to which poetry often resorts.

—Joseph Brodsky. From his essay "In the Shadow of Dante." You think you can put this shit over on me? Your entire brain fits in mine—with room to spare, in fact.

—You think if you could eradicate Christ from your life, if you could—

—*What?*

—purge your language of the word "God," you would be—not happy, you're not quite that stupid—but at least less split, more clearly and honestly *you*. You would get to the ground of Being and write honestly out of that, or live honestly in the silence such reduction required.

—Is that supposed to be something I didn't know? Are you declaring your independence?

—But you also think that if you could truly live with and for Jesus Christ, if you could purge your language of every lie that tells you this is not possible, you would be less split, more clearly and honestly *you*. You would get to the ground of Being and write honestly out of that, or live honestly in the silence such release required.

—This is not what we were talking about.

—It's the only subject. One doesn't put that kind of pressure on literature, or have those sorts of expectations (that, essentially, it will leave a trace, that it will in fact save you) unless there is spiritual anguish churning deep under the surface. This must be that extra part of your mind you mention. The water image in your poem is probably perfect in this regard, though I have the sneaking suspicion that this is coming as a revelation to you.

—Did you know I have an honorary doctorate in dementia?

—I'm not surprised. By the information or the segue. But go on.

—It was some corn college in the Midwest. Literally: it was surrounded by cornfields in every direction, fifteen miles from the nearest town. It was one of those earnest and overprogrammed affairs when you realize early on you've made a terrible mistake; I was pretty much trapped on campus for two days. Nothing to report from that. Do you believe that poetry is prayer? Is poetry a dying art? Is despair a perk or a preexisting condition? That sort of thing. Anyway, I was to be awarded the honorary degree at the end of the final event, which took place in a lecture hall that held maybe three hundred people. I had already been warned that they had forgotten to order me a robe and stole, so the president of the college would be loaning me his old one. Though I had spent part of the day with the man, it had not yet occurred to me that he was roughly seven inches taller than I am, and that his height might present some sartorial absurdities. The sleeves swallowed my

222

hands and the robe dragged the ground like a bridal train. I looked like Paddington the bear. The president and I stood in front of the crowd and went through the whole rigmarole, just the two of us, at the end of which he handed me my honorary doctorate. It was a year later before I noticed—actually, it was my wife who noticed—that I'd been honored for my "internationally recognized work in gerontology and dementia." Calculation or accident? Mistake by an overworked secretary or a gentle tip from the Paraclete? I never looked into it. I must say, it did make the whole trip seem worthwhile.

—(silence)

—Well, okay, it's not some deathless story or something. In fact it's quite deathful, given the degree I got.

—(silence)

—Okay, okay, telling a story about a botched honorary doctorate is inevitably a kind of humblebrag, but I figured you of all people would know I'm immune from that.

—(silence)

—You have become so humorless.

—Is that really all you remember from that weekend?

—I had a hell of a time procuring bourbon.

—She was in her late thirties, early forties. Two kids, nine and twelve. She was pretty but pasty, more like a memory of pretty, and had that distant intimate look of a soul in recession. You know what that's like. When the world withdraws from you, and you withdraw from yourself, but then how suffering can suddenly catalyze an intimacy that ordinary life would have prohibited, and how that's Christ alive between you, you and the other person, yes, but also the multiple yous that you are. As you may even have written once or twice.

—(silence)

223

—She wasn't there because she particularly liked poetry and might not have even been able to name one poem of yours. But she'd read something you'd published somewhere about cancer and Christ and made her way through the cornfields, not to test its authenticity but to be more directly touched by it, to feel it on her pulse, you might say, or, less poetically, to see if the hope it had sparked in her was mere words. Is any of this sounding familiar?

—She had a brain tumor.

—Yes. And what did you tell her?

—I don't know. What did I tell her?

—All morning gently swimming in the misery of a dead writer.

—I don't get it.

—We are what we are only in our last bastions. The knowledge of love and the knowledge of death are the same, and neither is knowledge.

—I have done my best to immortalize what I have failed to keep.

—Brodsky. Enough with the games. You didn't go to some corn college in the middle of Kansas or Michigan or wherever it was to pick up an honorary degree. You didn't go for money or a pathetic injection of adulation or because you wanted to get away from your chaotic domestic life. You went to have those ten minutes with that woman. Remember? You were trying to get your robe off when she walked up to you. You were already thinking of how you'd relate this event to friends.

—What did I *say* to her?

—There is a pain so—utter— / It swallows substance up—

—Oh come on—

—Then covers the Abyss with Trance—

—I never would have—

224

—So memory can step / Around—across—upon it— / As one within a Swoon—

—She's dead isn't—

—Goes safely—where an open eye— / Would drop him

—I have done my best—

—Bone by bone—

IFS ETERNALLY

Who could guess that one of life's most piercing discoveries would be a kind of edgeless entropy, this feeling—or is it a *lack* of feeling?—slowly creeping into all the crannies of your conscious-ness, a kind of claustrophobic panic that neither the events of your life, nor the people therein, nor the whole "million-petaled flower of being here" have added up to anything at all? What is the final revelation that life grants you? That there will be no final revelation.

> There is no steady unretracing progress in this life; we do not advance through fixed gradations, and at the last one pause:—through infancy's unconscious spell, boyhood's thoughtless faith, adolescence' doubt (the common doom), then scepticism, then disbelief, resting at last in manhood's pondering repose of If. But once gone through, we trace the round again; and are infants, boys, and men, and Ifs eternally.

> **Herman Melville, *Moby-Dick***

Fair enough. A clear-eyed acknowledgment of this fact seems to me both bracing and necessary. And insufficient. The revelation we want—or at any rate the revelation we need—is not ultimate, but intimate. There is no culmination that a life is heading toward, no blaze of radiance of which all our itchy intuitions and perishable epiphanies have been but sparks. Revelations there are, though. Those intuitions and epiphanies are real, and our reactions to them can be, in the moment, so total and unselfconscious that they warrant the name of—if they need a name at all—faith. But they fade, those moments, and we relapse into the vertiginous Ifs we are. What one wants as one grows older is some assurance that between the endless errands that crush the soul and the sudden warbler that ignites it, between the bills and births and meals and funerals, all the graces and losses of any life attended to no matter how erratically or imperfectly—under it all there *must* exist some intact tissue of meaning. Not meaning such as one might fully articulate or grasp, but a deep instinctive sense, an *assurance*, that in the incorrigibly plural swirl of life there abides some singularity of being, however fleeting its presence.

SNOW

The room was suddenly rich and the great bay-window was
Spawning snow and pink roses against it
Soundlessly collateral and incompatible:
World is suddener than we fancy it.

World is crazier and more of it than we think,
Incorrigibly plural. I peel and portion
A tangerine and spit the pips and feel
The drunkenness of things being various.

And the fire flames with a bubbling sound for world
Is more spiteful and gay than one supposes—

On the tongue on the eyes on the ears in the palms of one's
    hands—
There is more than glass between the snow and the huge
    roses.

Louis MacNeice

This poem is balanced between reception and perception, be-
tween the sensory intuitions/epiphanies out of which any sense of
existential unity emerges and the formulations of reality made by
the mind. These latter perceptions are not detached from reality—
the poet is, like any responsible philosopher or theologian, in it
up to his eyeballs—but they are secondary. I take the "more than"
of the last line to be a reference to consciousness, which both
connects us to, and separates us from, reality. To say that there
is more than glass between the snow (chaos) and the huge roses
(artificially created and sustained, an image of human beauty*) is
both to celebrate and lament an instant when this seemed not to
be the case.

It's the form of art that enables perception here. The percep-
tion is of chaos, at least from any singular human perspective,
an existence so various that the human mind will never master
it (there is *more* than glass/consciousness between the snow and
the huge roses). And yet that incorrigible plural has been, if not
mastered, at least entered; if not understood, at least undergone.
And one's vision has changed: the poem becomes a lens through
which we see all that we are unable to see. An acknowledgment
of this limitation/revelation is the basis of—the ground for—faith.
I wouldn't necessarily say that a denial of this vision and its im-

---

* Though of course the image is also "natural," as is any element of the "human."

plications is a denial of God. (The word "God," too, can be both accomplishment and failure, but is only sometimes, the rarest times, what it really ought to be, a beautiful fusion of both.) What I would say, though, is that a denial of this transcendent vision is a denial of reality itself. And since any individual life is part of that reality, as chaotically atomic as snow and roses, why should it be a surprise that we are Ifs eternally? A single tangerine ("I spit the pips") is enough to inspire—and then to defeat—a philosophy of life.

———

> Let me not have a life to look at, the way we look
> at a life we build to look at, in the world belief
> gives us to understand, a snowman life.

William Bronk, "On *Credo Ut Intelligam*"[*]

———

The thing about Christians, says the philosopher Alain, is that looking them in the eyes one senses that *they* don't believe it. This is, in my experience and apart from the obviously insane, accurate. But so is the reverse: look deep in the eyes of the avid atheist and you sense a quiver in the iron cage of conviction, a tiny—but ineradicable—*If*.

———

[*] I know, I know, I quoted this earlier. But you'd already forgotten it, hadn't you, my fellow If?

Terrence Malick's film *The Tree of Life* attempts to give a picture of wholeness that counters the modern sense of absolute atomization and—because of that sense—anomie. Thus the movement in that film from scenes of ordinary domestic life to cosmic creation, from a howling baby to a hungry dinosaur, from the startling, stabbing particularity of childhood to the soft gauze of a not-quite-credible heaven. This effort toward cumulative vision is conspicuous in the film, perhaps too much so at times, but what is most memorable about *Tree of Life* in the end is not its unified vision, but the intuition it enables (and it must remain an intuition) that all of life and creation might inhere, and cohere, within an instant—and that the instant is, so to speak, imperishable; it remains not simply accessible to memory but viscerally available. Memory, trauma experts tell us, is a matter of nerves. It changes our DNA, and its effects can survive not only our accidental unconsciousness and willful oblivion, but even our physical deaths. The sins of the fathers, it turns out, are quite literally visited upon the children, whose cells retain traces of traumas that never happened to them. (The studies that address this transmission all seem to focus on negative experience, but must we assume that our moments of extreme joy do not echo in the gleeful shrieks of our children's children?) It's not the wholeness of scale or scope one feels in the wake of Malick's movie, but the wholeness of these minute and immense, these joyful and terrifying, these discrete and seamless scraps of reality. In the long middle sections of the film set in central Texas, it's as if time were tangible, as if childhood were a substance you could touch and taste and—herein lies the film's greatness— never lose.

———

Never lose? Most people believe that one of the reliefs (facile distortions, the atheist would say) that religion promises is just the kind of panoptic vision I've been talking about. Religion is the very thing that puts all of our experiences in context; it makes life *mean*. But in fact this is just what faith ought to free a person from: the *need* for this kind of seeing, the compulsion to believe that there is *one truth*. This is in fact the stale hell of modern scientific materialism, which is by no means confined to science.

> In all the thoughts, feelings, and ideas which I form about anything, there is wanting the something universal which could bind all these together in one whole. Each feeling and each thought lives detached in me, and in all my opinions about science, the theater, literature, and my pupils, and in all the little pictures which my imagination paints, not even the most cunning analyst will discover what is called the general idea, or the god of the living man. And if this is not there, then nothing is there. In poverty such as this, a serious infirmity, fear of death, influence of circumstances and people would have been enough to overthrow and shatter all that I formerly considered as my conception of the world, and all wherein I saw the meaning and joy of my life.

Anton Chekhov, "A Boring Story,"
tr. by Richard Pevear and Larissa Volokhonsky

What Chekhov is saying (through his character Nikolai Stepanovich, though the identification seems pretty seamless) is that, for the person who believes we are completely reducible to physiological firings in the brain, and that we are essentially pinnacle insects, impressive, yes, prone to deviations both endearing and alarming, most definitely, but in the end as rote and reactionary as the immense machine through which we move and live and have our algebraic being—for such a person, any setback to the steady pleasure of a prosperous and emotionally gratifying existence, much less any real tragedy such as the prospect of our own deaths or the death of someone we "love" (for a scientific materialist, the word must always be in quotes) blows open the doors of deliberate ignorance behind which we were hiding: the real meaning of our lives comes flooding in, which is that there is no real meaning to our lives whatsoever.

The contemporary reaction to this state of affairs is mostly either willful obliviousness, frenetic activity, or despair. (And of course these may be inseparable from each other.) Chekhov's reaction, according to Lev Shestov, was the only possible honorable reaction available to an artist who has committed himself to "creation out of the void":

> But how shall a man struggle with materialism? And can it be overcome? Perhaps Chekhov's method may seem strange to my reader, nevertheless it is clear that he came to the conclusion that there was only one way to struggle, to which the prophets of old turned themselves: to beat one's head against the wall.

Penultimate Words and Other Essays

This frustrated energy is what I feel in every single Chekhov story or play (Alice Munro is a modern inheritor), the implacability of a force that is both stronger and weaker than fate: stronger, because it doesn't offer any kind of coherent act or agency either to align oneself with or to resist; weaker, because for anyone who actually lives out the consequences of one's belief, it elicits not awe but entropy, not rage but resignation.

———

Shestov's comparison with the prophets is misguided, I think, though it's accidentally illuminating. The wall Chekhov beat his head against was existential—essentially the Void. The wall the prophets beat their heads against was humanity. God was a given, his existence so woven into their own that they could speak with his voice. "It is not a world devoid of meaning that evokes the prophet's consternation," writes Abraham Joshua Heschel, "but a world deaf to meaning." What Chekhov sought, in the passage above and elsewhere, was respite, some solid ground on which to stand and survey the whole of life. It is, essentially, a desire to step outside of time, which, as Heschel says, is "devoid of poise."* For the prophetic imagination, though, there is no "outside," and the meaning of time will never be realized by denying or evading its nature. To understand this dynamic, and one's place in it, is not to "understand" God, but it can enable (Heschel again) "moments in which the mind peels off, as it were, its not-knowing. Thought is like touch, comprehending by being comprehended." It doesn't matter that you believe in such connections; what matters is that you apprehend them. And live up to them. Such moments, and the subsequent allegiance to them that sometimes goes by the name of faith, can free one from the circular despair articulated by Melville and Chekhov.

———

* Heschel actually says that "history is devoid of poise," but he clearly means to include the current moment and thus all of time.

Why am I making so much of this one comparison? Because I feel that I—and many others—might be indicted by it. My instinct is to hold up something like that Louis MacNeice poem above as one of these moments when the mind peels off its not-knowing. Yet there is a sense in which the poem, for all its attestations of multiplicity and chaos, operates from within a position of (factitious) poise, or a position in which poise is at least a possibility. The lyric instant, the form that makes the perception possible, implicitly asserts an order that the poem explicitly denies. "Snow" is a deeply spiritual poem (whatever MacNeice "believed"). As with the Kamieńska poem I quoted in the first entry of this book, one feels currents of reality usually imperceptible to us rippling through the wrought iron of its lines. But the poem is not prophetic in Heschel's sense. It takes the relationship between spirit and matter as a good, but not as a given.

Perhaps the very *need* to perceive some overarching meaning to one's life is simply one more compulsion for control, and not a sign of spiritual health but of pathology, the same need to control that has decimated nature, volatilized every racial and gender relation, and locked God into holy books and human institutions. I suspect the very way I have framed this entire issue—the moment versus the flux, the sensation versus the formulation, the bright particular versus the incorrigibly plural—is itself too mired in a literary and intellectual history to admit of—much less enable—other options.

———

I do not want a poem
that depends on madness alone
for its vision, nor on madness
alone for its madness.

Having made my meaning,
I make my meaning
clear. It is unreal
like the wings of ants.

Ralph Dickey, "The Arcanum Poems"

Teasing out the difference between madness and vision can be a difficult enterprise for poets. And for prophets. And for anyone who has experienced—and lived to doubt—the presence of God.

Dickey's poem is a statement *about* the moment of madness/vision rather than the thing itself. It's the equivalent of criticism, or theology, or any ex post facto attempt at understanding revelation. And yet there it sits, looking for all the world like a poem, and with a glinting gem of obliquity at its heart which itself cries out for critical explanation. If you've made your meaning, why the need to make it clear? Oh, and: *unreal / like the wings of ants*?

In fact, some species of ants *do* have wings, though they appear only during the reproductive stage when an ant is seeking a mate. I feel sure Dickey was in possession of this knowledge. Might his poem be saying, then, (and I do think it's the poem speaking, not the poet's idea encoded within it) that meaning is real only when it is reproduced—only, that is, when it makes its way from one mind to another. "How little and how impotent a piece of the world is any man alone?" asks John Donne. When I think of the consciousness that generates the circular sorrow of "Ifs eternally," or the one trying to find the one thing that will unify all the disparate experiences of one life, I think of a man—almost always a man, though there are notable exceptions—sitting alone in a room and doggedly trying to *figure it all out*. I read Dickey's poem as a way out of that. It is two minds that make meaning, which is an action, not a fact, or is at least catalyzed by relation, however rooted it may be in one brain. "For where two or three are gathered together in my name," Jesus promised, "there am I in the midst of them." A poem is a place where two or three can gather, and a place where revelation and explanation are not separate from each other.

———

Ralph Dickey died of suicide at the age of twenty-eight. A poem may be a locus for spiritual connection and comfort, but it's not sufficient. Let us not pretend time is not howling outside, even now, nor that the walls we make, even these, will long withstand it.

———

Can there ever be reconcilement between the confusion of self and the vision of truth? Between the chaos of our days and the glimpses of order and love upon which we stake our faith? Between the *If* and the *Is*?

LOVE SONG

First came cancer of the liver, then came the man
leaping from bed to floor and crawling around
on all fours, shouting: "Leave me alone, all of you,
just leave me be," such was his pain without remission.
Then came death and, in that zero hour, the shirt missing
           a button.
I'll sew it on, I promise,
   but wait, let me cry first.

"Ah," said Martha and Mary, "if You had been here,
our brother would not have died." "Wait," said Jesus,
"let me cry first."
So it's okay to cry? I can cry too?
If they asked me now about life's joy,
I would only have the memory of a tiny flower.
Or maybe more, I'm very sad today:
what I say, I unsay. But God's Word
is the truth. That's why this song has the name it has.

Adélia Prado

"Let me cry first" is not in fact what Jesus said at the death of Laza-rus. He didn't say anything at all in the moment of that particular verse, which is famous for being the shortest verse in the Bible: "Jesus wept." The least words for the largest sorrow. It's hardly a paradox.

What is a paradox, though, is that Jesus weeps even though he knows what is going to happen: he will raise Lazarus from the dead. His knowledge spares him nothing. It's almost as if "what is going to happen" is *contingent* upon human grief, as if fact had to pass through feeling in order to be fact. That the fact here is a miracle only intensifies the strangeness.

We know how, in psychological terms, time can get stuck in the mind and life of someone who has not learned to properly grieve. The scene with Jesus suggests that time itself becomes sclerotic without proper sorrow. What is "proper sorrow"? "I'll sew it on, I promise, / but wait, let me cry first." Or: "If they asked me now about life's joy / I would have only the memory of a tiny flower." The loose button on the shirt of a dying man, the memory of a tiny flower in the face of annihilating pain—the details scald with irony and irrelevance. And then they burn with love. The poem is not saying that the button and the flower and grief and God's love are "related" to each other. It's saying they *are* each other. In the terms of this essay, the *if* is the resurrection this poem implies ("God's word is the truth"). The *is* is the button. The *if* is what any honest faith looks like in this life. The *is* is the memory of a tiny flower. And they are all, for anyone fortunate enough to feel it, inseparable.

There is something both accidental and necessary, both salvaged and given, about these details and the vision of life that emerges from the poem. A whole new relation to reality seems possible. The Biblical scholar Walter Brueggemann says that what true prophetic witness enables is just such genuine newness. (This is what distinguishes such witness/voice from the head-beating-on-the-wall method of Chekhov.) We don't want newness, though, not really. "It puts us next to the 'therefore' of God," as Brueggemann says, which might cost us our comforts and achievements, our treasured despairs. It might cost us, us. "Nothing but grief could permit newness. Only a poem could bring the grief to notice." Both true. Both ambiguous gifts of God. And *that's* why Prado's poem—and this essay, and this whole damn book—all have the names they have.

42

I SANG PAIN

I sang pain
back of Mr. Derek's listing shed.
There were no words,
or words were what the cold ground,
the split timber,
and the sometime slime
of caterpillar or molasses grasshopper
said.
    Dark came,
all swathe and crow,
solid as what we know
and know not to utter,
later.
    Years they were,
rustle and skirr—
mesquite beans? rabbit?
The ground was dry.
The ground was wet.

If you ask me who I am,
how I live and what god I serve,
I have no answer. But once,
behind a disused shed,

in thrall to an untranslatable power,
I was myself, and I cried silence
adequate to the hour.

43

A MAMMAL'S NOTEBOOK

The kind of Christianity to which I adhere allows itself to be distinguished as one religion among others on the map of "dispersion" and "confusion" after Babel; after Babel does not designate some catastrophe, but rather the mere assertion of the plurality characteristic of all human phenomena. Relativism, if one wishes. I accept this external judgment. However, for me, living it from within, my adhesion is absolute, is noncomparable, not radically chosen, not arbitrarily posited. I cling to inserting the predicate "relative" in the phrase "relative absolute" in order to inscribe into the vow of adhesion the mark of an original chance, raised to the rank of a destiny by a continuous choice.

Paul Ricoeur, *Living Up to Death*

Human beings are called upon to live in their inmost region and to have themselves as much in hand as is possible only from that center point; only from there can they rightly come to terms with the world. Only from there can they find the place in the world that has been intended for them. In all of this, they can never *see through* this inmost region completely. It is God's mystery, which God alone can reveal to the degree that pleases him.

Edith Stein, *The Science of the Cross*

Many poets are not poets for the same reason that religious men and women are not saints; they never succeed in being themselves. They never get around to being the particular poet or the particular monk they are intended to be by God. They never become the man or the artist who is called for by all the circumstances of their life. They waste their years in vain efforts to be some other poet or some other saint.

Thomas Merton, *New Seeds of Contemplation*

To lift, without ever asking what animal exactly it once
  belonged to,
the socketed helmet that what's left of the skull equals
up to your face, to hold it there, mask-like, to look through it
  until
looking through means looking back, back through the skull,
into the self that is partly the animal you've always wanted
  to be,
that—depending—fear has prevented or rescued you from
  becoming,
to know utterly what you'll never be, to understand in
  doing so
what you are, and say no to it, not to who you are, to say no
  to despair.

Carl Phillips, "Gold Leaf"

. . . truly God's finger touching the very vein of personality, which nothing else can reach and man can respond to by no play whatever, by bare acknowledgement only, the counter stress which God alone can feel . . . the aspiration in answer to his inspiration.

Gerard Manley Hopkins, *Letters*

Slowly death turns up the lights from underneath, from the
    ground. The heath shines, a stronger and stronger purple—
no, a color no one has seen . . . until the morning's pale light
    whines in through the eyelids

and I wake to that unshakeable PERHAPS that carries me
    through the wavering world.
And each abstract picture of the world is as impossible as the
    blueprint of a storm.

Tomas Tranströmer, "Brief Pause in the Organ Recital,"
tr. by Robin Fulton

Belief in God is an inclination to listen,
but as we grow older and our freedom hardens,
we hardly even want to hear ourselves . . .

Robert Lowell, "No Hearing"

To be interested in Satie, one must be disinterested to begin with, accept that a sound is a sound and a man is a man, give up illusions about ideas of order, expressions of sentiment, and all the rest of our inherited claptrap.

John Cage, *Silence: Lectures and Writings*

When I was young people used to say to me "Wait until you're fifty. You'll see." I am fifty. I haven't seen anything.

Erik Satie, A *Mammal's Notebook*

The butterfly, the cabbage white,
(His honest idiocy of flight)
Will never now, it is too late,
Master the art of flying straight,
Yet has—who knows so well as I?—
A just sense of how not to fly:
He lurches here and here by guess
And God and hope and hopelessness.
Even the aerobatic swift
Has not his flying-crooked gift.

Robert Graves, "Flying Crooked"

I DON'T BELIEVE IN THE SOUL

The quick flints avid at the feeder.
The bare trees like dendrites intuiting blue.
The burl that, looked at, blurs into a squirrel.
The little nonetheless that keep me you.

WHAT THE WESTERN MYSTIC

What the Western mystic,
Meister Eckhart,
called

the silent desert
of the divinity
calls

to the human spirit
as do the empty spaces
of earth and sky,

even to the point
of self-negation.
But when exploration

turns to love
the heart longs
not for extinction

but exchange,
not for union
but communion.*

---

* This is a found poem extracted verbatim from John V. Taylor's *The Christlike God*. All I have done is lineate his original text.

46

MY CHRIST

I.

Of course there can be no such thing. My Christ. Two thousand years of permutations, interpretations, hardcore seminars and wholesale slaughters. *My* Christ?

Of course there can only be such a thing. He is a universal language that only an individual heart can translate. *My* Christ.

I begin this entry prompted by two things, a passage in C. S. Lewis's *The Great Divorce* in which he talks of the necessity of drinking one's particular shame to the dregs if one would ever be released from it. My shame is Christianity, sometimes. My shame is myself, sometimes. In any event I too often too-timidly sip of both, savoring my spite.

The second thing? As I read the Lewis passage a hawk flew into my vision and landed on a tree limb I can see from my study. How we want the world to speak to us! But some utterance is too intrinsic to be speech. Some luck is love incompletely seen.

II.

"Love"? The word assumes that the necessity that creates and crushes at the same time, sometimes in the same act, is not quite that—necessity, that is; that the ineluctability of the laws of matter is only apparent; that the blind force has feeling. And feeling that is by no means blind, for the mind behind it seems to reach right into my study in Hamden, Connecticut, August 6, 2021, to be perceived by the hungry and often hapless mind of a writer eager to see meaning in molecules, incarnation and resurrection in a random raptor.

III.

Incarnation? Resurrection? Why these leaps? Why not let the world be world, for Christ's sake, luck be luck? Because "the force that through the green fuse drives the flower / drives my green age" (Dylan Thomas). Because "there are things we live among, and to know them / is to know ourselves" (George Oppen). Because the connection between us and the world is both absolute and absolutely contingent. We know in our bones that this is so, and sacred, and we know in our bones that we can never *know* that this is so, and that lack is also sacred. My Christ is both the means and the meaning of matter.

And the latter (not greater) miracle, resurrection? Why make *that* leap? It is life that brings one to believe in the incarnation, though "believe" is a neutered word for the mutual indwelling I have just described. It is life that teaches us of love, and "it is love," as Wittgenstein said in his last book, "that believes in the resurrection." That love is not possessed, not controlled, never fully understood—this is one lesson any truly attentive life teaches (*love* believes in the resurrection; one's will is not relevant); that love is more than human is another, whether it's some carnal connection leading one to "the love that moves the sun and the other stars" (Dante) or some rapturous merging with eternity that leaves one, like Julian of Norwich, holding all creation compacted into a hazelnut.

My Christ—probably not tall, certainly not white, obviously not Christian, dirty and ragged as any impoverished and itinerant first-century minister would have been—lifts up his arms and says (to me, here in Hamden with my plump doubts and taloned falcon): "And all things, whatsoever ye shall ask in prayer, believing, ye shall receive."

IV.

How in the world to hear this? It's either transparently false, because I think instantly of two people I knew whose faith seemed to me bone-deep and unimpeachable even as they were mercilessly crushed by cancers which they at every minute believed God would heal; or it's a kind of trick scripture, guarded by a seed of sophistry, because in every failed instance a blindly pious observer can say, "Well, they must not have truly *believed* in the possibility that their prayers would be answered."

What if the verse—here, now, in the twenty-first century—is both more and less literal than it seems? Scripture is no more static than electrons are. Its meaning depends on your position in space and time. If you ask with such attention as you are able, then, such attention as you have been given; and if you ask, not of "God" exactly but of *things* (which makes perfect, even superior, grammatical sense), then you will receive reality, which means—here, now, in the twenty-first century—that you will be received into reality. It's not a new idea. "That the self advances and realizes the ten thousand things is delusion. That the ten thousand things advance and realize the self is enlightenment."*

---

* Dogen, *Genjo Koan*

The wrist of the afterlife curls around
A stem. Immortality comes first
If ever it comes afterwards. Suffer
The rebuke and move on, which is to say
Upwards into the sainted, oldest tree.

Donald Revell, "A Hint to Plotinus"

However mysterious the mind-body problem may be for us, we
    should always
remember that it is a solved problem for nature.

Erik C. Banks

Is it? Solved, that is? Many thinkers have written about the possibility that the human mind is nature becoming conscious of itself. I wouldn't limit the adjective to "human," as consciousness seems to me a continuum, evident in apes and whales, for instance, but also uncanny kindred in volatile rocks and communicating roots. But let that be for the moment. If humans are inextricably a part of nature, and if humans are still wracked with anxieties and difficulties (spiritual, intellectual, psychological) arising from an unresolved tension between the mind and the brain (this is what Banks means), then it follows that this "problem" is hardly solved within some separate or even overarching entity called "nature."

The theoretical physicist Carlo Rovelli, in his most recent book *Helgoland*, has posited a theory that erases the distinction between the human mind and the natural world.* The fact that observing the action of quantum particles influences the way they behave is well-established. Rovelli says that quantum theory has hitherto been limited in thinking of this dynamic only in relation to us, when in fact quantum theory "describes how every physical object manifests itself to any other physical object. How any physical entity acts on *any* other physical entity." This leads to a radical conclusion, his "relational theory," which, if correct, upends the history of physics (and other fields as well):

> The discovery of quantum theory, I believe, is the discovery that the properties of any entity are nothing other than the way in which that entity influences others. It exists only through its interactions. Quantum theory is the theory of how things influence each other. And this is the best description of nature that we have.

Existence is relation. Full stop. If you cannot tell anything about how an object is relating to what is around it, then *poof*, there is no object. This is incontrovertible at the micro level. That it seems not to obtain at the macro level has led to many theories, some quite imaginatively provocative (the "multiverse" is the best known) but all, according to Rovelli, requiring that we posit realities we can never observe—a leap of faith, if you will. For Rovelli, the micro and the macro mean one thing, which is nothing. Billions and billions of quantum phenomena are happening around us (and in us!) at every instant. Our life, our need to make meaning from it,

---

* Rovelli—confusingly, I think—quotes Erik C. Banks's philosophical conclusion with approval.

is all a kind of blindness. "The solidity of the classical vision of the world is nothing other than our own myopia. The certainties of classical physics are just probabilities. The well-defined and solid picture of the world given by the old physics is an illusion . . . Centuries of Western speculation on the subject, and on the nature of consciousness, vanish like morning mist."

A despairing vision? Not for Rovelli. "There is a sense of the vertiginous—of freedom, happiness, lightness—in the vision of the world that we are offered by the discovery of quanta . . . Watching what appeared to be as solid as rock melt into air makes lighter, it seems to me, the transitory and bittersweet flowing of our lives." Gone is the scientific and philosophical materialism and determinism that have choked the soul for the last century. If everything is its relation to other things, the future can hardly be fixed, no matter how refined one's understanding of the laws of matter are. (The hawk really is "random.") For Rovelli this represents the end of metaphysics, which has been gumming up the works between the mind ("brain," I guess he would say) and reality for so many centuries. He would be surprised and perhaps appalled, then, to learn that a religious person might feel as light and liberated by his vision as he does. Yet I do. Not only does it align with many of the artists and thinkers I have quoted in this book,* it seems to me perfectly *trinitarian* in its implications. The "veil upon veil" that opens endlessly forever—this is God. The world that we still live very much in the midst of, the illusory rocks that slice us open and the faces made of infinitesimal and untouchable grains that we touch and love with everything we are—this is Jesus on the earth. He, too,

---

* Kandinsky: "The world sounds. It is a cosmos of spiritually affective beings. Thus dead matter is living spirit."

was made of these grains; he, too, left not a wrack behind. And the elation that both Rovelli and I feel when we are so moved by this emptiness that is a fullness, this lack that feels so like love—this is the Holy Spirit working in ever new ways through the mix of time and timelessness that is our birthright. And none of this "exists" unless and until you turn your full attention to it.

VII.

Overingenious? I really don't think so. Overingenious *for me* (and my Christ)? Probably.

On a podcast for a Jewish magazine recently one of the hosts told me—querulously, it seemed to me, which, given history, given me, seemed fair—that he could understand from my writings why I was a theist but not why I was a *Christian*. All my thoughts about incarnation and resurrection, apophasis and cataphasis, atoms and Adams—*poof*—gone. I stammered out the only answer I had. I am a Christian because once when I was suffering terribly and near death Christ came to me—in my mind, in my heart, through the minds and hearts of others, through what I was reading and what I was touching and tasting and seeing, he seemed everywhere dammit—and was present in my soul. *Was* my soul.

I've fallen so far from that time. I don't relish, and often don't even recognize, "Christianity." And still, my Christ has led me from that moment to this one, has patiently waited while I have thought and fought my way through all these disconnected fragments, both in this entry and in this book. My Christ, I think, is disappointed that I still think I can *think* my way through such things. That *through* is even the preposition that should occur to me here.

VIII

One life, not one among
A thousand others of quail
Like tipsy mandarins crowding
The cold of a low wall
Along a line of trees, the angel
Promised me and nothing
More, nothing to weigh.

Menippus and Lucian
Be with me now as I
Feel my way among
Misted pillars and ghosts
Of breath on upper Broadway.
A quick kiss in the crosswalk is
More to me than mankind.

There is no middle ground.
There is our empty bench.
There is the stoop of pigeons.
Either I have been alone
Every hour of my life or
Never once, not even
One moment, and the mist rising.

Donald Revell, *"Senesco Sed Amo"*

WOMAN, WITH TOMATO

Men want mystery when the meanings are plain.
Never a bird by chance or a yawn a yawn.
The very cur can't beg or bolt a yolk
without morning being aboil with creation.
God forbid a meager leaf should golden.
Men want life and love to spill out of themselves
(unless the love's too voluptuously alive, of course),
want roots to clutch and buds to bell, want want.
You wonder why I salt my slices one by one,
why I sit, alone, in my slice of sun.
Men want mystery when the meanings are plain.

THE EFT

Not nothingness but too many meanings
as of a creature under siege.
First the basement floods the first day of the year
and instead of making love we make rage.
Then the kids lava down into the living room,
the dog vomits up something from the Pleistocene,
and in the brick wind the whole house tilts and lists like . . .
like an old house.
                    "Any problem that can be solved with money
is not a problem," bubbles up from somewhere,
as if that weren't our honeymoon—eight days in a rainforest,
the howling darks and vehement greens—floating in the murk,
as if that weren't—in a Connecticut suburb, in winter—a snake
that just breached and vanished in the corner,
and as if this wisdom weren't merely the echo of an uncle
whose only grace was goats, Liza and Little Bean,
Blue-Blue and Getchagone, all gone
to tuft and viscera, to an old man's only ever tears,
at the teeth of wild dogs.
                    Look at them,
our girls, bent over their project now
and impervious to everything. And look at you,
bent over the sump pump's guts

in your brand-new and barely tethered Christmas robe,
smoothing sockets, exquisiting screws and lug nuts
like a lissome clockmaker.
                              I go down
into the flood again to find—among the floating bows
and ornaments, the party plates and drowned dolls—a Jesus lizard
leisurely eating thirteen three-inch caterpillars
from the side of a cocobolo tree.
Remember? Its placid appetency, its face full of hills,
the way time warped and distended like heat
as it looked right through the camera's lens,
philosophically chomping each green glob.
"If you will accept it, if you will drink the cup to the bottom—
you will find it nourishing: but try to do anything else with it
and it scalds." Remember? *The Great Divorce*.
Though our favorites were the dwarf and the tragedian,
who are one entity, actually, the latter the actor
of the former's pain, or after-image of pain, rather,
the pleasure pain becomes when it becomes a thing to wield,
a means of extracting meaning from someone else's heart
when your own has run dry.
                              "Let's try it now,"
you say, clomping downstairs in bathrobe and rubber boots,
and it goes, of course it does, the motor and the water,
the anger and the hours, until we stand
in a dispensation we had not known we desired,
the purged clutter and the pristined concrete,
as if catastrophe were but occasion for a further order,
which might include, apparently, even a snake,
which even as we glimpse again
grows legs, swivels its suddenly unsnakelike head,

and is a newt—or an eft, rather—that trundles off
("Scoot, newt! Scoot, newt!" the girls encourage)
behind the freezer.
                    "Hell is a state of mind—
ye never said a truer word. And every state of mind,
left to itself, every shutting up of the creature
within the dungeon of its own mind—is, in the end, Hell.
But Heaven is not a state of mind. Heaven is reality itself.
All that is fully real is Heavenly."
                              Too tired to make love
we make love when the girls have gone to sleep
and go to sleep holding each other like buoys
as the waters drip and descend
from every slope and bend in the waterlogged land
of Connecticut, and the pump kicks on like a sound
so inside it's cellular, "for all that can be shaken will be shaken
and only the unshakeable remains."

49

THE CANCER CHAIR

We do not believe. We fear. *

The second worst thing about cancer chairs is that they are attached to televisions. Someone somewhere is always at war with silence. It's not possible to read anything serious, so I answer emails, or put on headphones and watch some cop drama on my computer, or, if it seems unavoidable, explore the lives of my nurses. A yearly trip to the Bahamas with old girlfriends, a costume party with political overtones, an advanced degree on the internet, a kid headed to college: They're all the same, these lives, which is to say of course that the nurses tell me nothing, perhaps because amid the din and pain it's impossible to say anything of substance, or perhaps because they know that nothing is precisely what we both expect. It's the very currency of the place. Perhaps they are in fact being excruciatingly candid.

There is a cancer camaraderie I've never felt. That I find inimical, in fact. Along with the official optimism that percolates out of pamphlets, the milestone celebrations that seem aimed at children, the lemonade that people squeeze out of their tumors. My stoniness has not always served me well. Among the cancer staff, there is special affection for the jocular sufferer, the one who

---

* Aua, an Inuk medicine man, as told to Knud Rasmussen, quoted in *Arctic Dreams* by Barry Lopez.

makes light of lousy bowel movements and extols the spiritual tonic of neuropathy. And why not? Spend your waking life in hell, and you too might cherish the soul who'd learned to praise the flames. I can't do it. I'm not chipper by nature, and just hearing the word "cancer" makes me feel like I'm wearing a welder's mask.

In the cancer chair there is always a pillow and a blanket. I've never used either, though there have been two occasions when my spastic reactions to my cure (2007, 2013) led nurses to hurriedly pile blankets on my feverish form in the way I pile blankets on my twin girls when they come down in the mornings and are cold. Now why did I have to think of that. The comparison, I mean. It is wildly inapt: the nurses' ministrations are efficient and mirthless, and not once have they concluded with a good tickle. Why must the mind—my mind—make these errant excavations into pure pain? I was just digging along like a dog, chats and chairs, a pillow and a blanket.

My children have never seen a cancer chair. They have visited me during extended hospital stays, but that's different, and the last one is just far back enough in their consciousness to be, for now, benign. They remember the brightly colored fish in the tank outside the dining hall, the modern waterfall down the flat marble in the lobby, and that every night I ordered an extra pudding and let them have both. All in all, great fun.

Often I see a dire child somewhere between the elevators and the blood cancer corner. The children's hospital is on the same floor. They are not all the same, these children. Not that I've ever spoken to one of them, nor learned one detail of their lives and predicaments, nor even, not for one instant, met their or their parents' eyes. Yet each sighting shocks the soul like a moment of negative grace, a kind of anti-inspiration, a little shard in the mind that there is no way to absorb or dislodge. There is nothing to remember, except the nothing I am unable to forget.

Today it was a bald boy of five or six poised at the door to the outdoor garden, one hand attached by tubes to his towering cancer tree, the other held by his mother, who was young, elegant in a way that suggested wealth, and in a kind of distress that seemed incomprehensible by its very banality. The boy couldn't decide whether he wanted to go out to the garden or not, and the moment had obviously escalated to a kind of crisis. Nietzsche says that not only is there no point to pity but it's actively malign. To feel your heart breaking at the sight of a tiny gray-faced boy trying to decide whether to go out to a rooftop garden or not—what does this do but secrete a little more misery into the atmosphere? I had my parking validated and my wrist banded and took a seat where I could not see them, the young mother and the old child. They went back into the children's hospital. (Are there miniature cancer chairs, I wonder?) Or they stood outside staring at the red cliffs of East Rock. I looked at my phone. I got a drink of water that I didn't want. Then the next name called was mine.

A group of cancer chairs is called a pod. I'm not sure if this is typical or specific to my hospital. There are five pods in just this corner of my floor (which is one of twelve), and all of them, near as I can tell, are occupied at every hour of every day. Sperm whales were once so numerous that a ship could sail all day in the opposite direction of a line of them and never reach the end. They are intelligent, musical, perhaps moral. In 2011 a pod of sperm whales adopted a deformed baby bottlenose dolphin, which his own kind had cast out, presumably because of his deformity. Moby Dick was a sperm whale. "That inscrutable thing is chiefly what I hate," says Ahab, "and be the white whale agent, or be the white whale principal, I will wreak that hate upon him." Whaling peaked in New England in the mid-nineteenth century, when thousands of young men (and the occasional disguised woman) sailed off in search of adventure, money, meaning. It was a dangerous trade. Voyages could last several years, and hunts often took place in bad weather, at night, or both. A whale catcher could lean to forty-five degrees in the chase, and sometimes, racing a fierce wind and with its upper rigging shining ice, the scales tilted and the whole crystal ship—and the twenty or so bright lives aboard—went dark.

Whales evolved from land mammals. In essence, evolution reversed itself, and the creature that had once crawled out of the sea to survive finally, and for the same reason, flopped leglessly back in. This is the sort of information that passes through the brain—or my brain—without leaving a trace, along with the fact that there are forty-six billion light-years between the edge of my cancer chair and the edge of the universe; or that a newborn infant has about sixty zettabytes of information swirling around inside her (all the digital information in the world adds up to roughly forty zettabytes); or that in the thirty seconds it will take you to read this sentence there will have been sixty million successful cell divisions within your beloved body. Or not. I've known two apparently healthy people who died within a month of their diagnoses. One minute they were planning dinner, talking on the phone, stalking holidays. Then the crystal ship.

Each cancer chair has two folding trays, one for the nurse's paraphernalia and one for the patient's. Today I need both sides to accommodate the materials I've accumulated for my lecture on Job in my class called Suffering. Have a hammer use a hammer. Not that this rote monthly infusion for my immune system constitutes suffering, unless you count the light roast coffee (I prefer dark), and the noise seeping into my noise-canceling earphones, and the fact that I don't know how to talk about suffering without talking about God, and I'm tired of talking about God. "Is it a how-to course?" a gently skewering wit asked me when I was describing the reading list. I laughed, or tried to, but when I told the story to my teaching partner, the theologian Miroslav Volf, he said soberly, "Damn right it is." A few years ago I compiled an anthology of poems about joy, and as I've been thinking about suffering, it has occurred to me that the two abstractions are alike in at least four ways:

1. They are never abstract.
2. They are inevitable. (I don't believe any life is entirely devoid of joy.)
3. They cannot be willed or instrumentalized. (Thus I am excluding any pain that is initiated to serve an end.)
4. There is something sacred in them, or at least there can be.

It's this last assertion that sticks in the modern throat. For most people suffering is simply something to avoid thinking about for as long as possible, and then, because to avoid it forever is impossible, to expunge from one's mind the minute one is beyond the scald. Think of our culture's almost Talmudic attention to physical health or—adjusting the dial on Oblivion ever so slightly—our national addiction to opiates. Think of all the hours we feed our brains to screens, the numb way we move from one month's mass shooting to the next. Think of the way we separate the very old from society as if they were being culled, the stifled, baffled air of the modern funeral. The proximate causes for these conditions are many, but the ultimate one, I suspect, is the same: we would evade our pain.

It wasn't always thus. "Pain which cannot forget falls drop by drop upon the heart, until in our own despite, against our will, comes wisdom to us from the awful grace of God." That's Aeschylus, writing roughly 2,500 years ago. Jump forward five hundred years and you have Saint Paul: "But rejoice insofar as you share Christ's sufferings, that you may also rejoice and be glad when his glory is revealed." A quick spin of the globe and a skip of a millennium and there's Rumi: "The wound is the place where the Light enters you." Montaigne: "A man who fears suffering is already suffering from what he fears." Still too far back? Proust: "We are healed of a suffering only by experiencing it to the full." Dickinson: "He deposes Doom / Who hath suffered him." Nietzsche: "The discipline of suffering, of great suffering—know ye not that it is only this discipline that has produced all of the elevations of humanity hitherto?"

But what if circumstances—and humanity—really have recently changed? This is the thesis of Yuval Noah Harari's ominously titled book *Homo Deus*. Humanity has crossed a threshold, he argues, and is on the verge of removing some traditional forms of suffering from the existential equation altogether.

> Having reduced mortality from starvation, disease and violence, we will now aim to overcome old age and even death itself. Having saved people from abject misery, we will now aim to make them positively happy. And having raised humanity above the beastly level of survival struggles, we will now aim to upgrade humans into gods, and turn *Homo sapiens* into *Homo deus*.

I hear Satan himself hissing these sentences ("Here grows the Cure of all, this Fruit Divine . . ."), but my strenuous revulsion came as a surprise to some of my students, who viewed Harari's argument not as a prediction but as a straightforward and accurate description of our current reality. We are at Yale, I suppose, and not in Syria,

Honduras, or some other part of the planet—much of New Haven, say—not inhabited by the Haves. But never mind the substance of the argument. That it *is* an argument, one taken quite seriously by people running the world—Barack Obama and Bill Gates are big fans—is the salient point. Let's assume Harari is right. What might that mean for us?

Death, I think. One less literal, but ultimately more fatal, than the one we fear. This is the world of Nietzsche's "Last Men," who have triumphed over the traditional agonies of existence and now bask in neutered happiness. For Nietzsche there can be no creativity without suffering, and there can be no life without creativity. Nor can one winnow out the highs and lows of one's life like wheat from tares. There is no (true) joy without suffering and there is no (meaningful) suffering without joy. "Joy wants eternity," Nietzsche says, and eternity is not escape from time but all time redeemed. To say yes to one moment in life is to say yes to all of them. To feel the joy of kissing your child on the cheek at night is to sanction, even to praise, the riot of cells rotting out the gray-faced boy outside the cancer garden.

My lines are obstructed. This happens fairly often, especially if I am trying to type. First there is a modest beeping from the middle of the cancer tree, then it grows louder if no nurse comes, until finally it rises to a shrill alarm that sends a current of articulate irritation between the eyes of the entire pod. I fiddle with the cancer controls on the cancer tree, but even after all these years I am helpless. Where the hell is Jessica, the prettiest nurse in the cancer pageant? What a stupid thing to say. Some days rage courses through me with the chemicals and all I want to do is defile.

In fact, I'm always relieved when I'm assigned to Jessica's station. It seems impossible, but on more than one occasion I have felt nothing at all when she inserted the line into my forearm. I like her placid manner, her Connecticut accent ("mittns"), her ambiguous glitter (her standard nurses' clogs are decorated with polka dots). I like the impersonal way she calls me "my friend," and the gentle jibes she'll sometimes let fall like testaments to ordinary life. What's it like to carry a face like hers (and "pretty" is not the right word) into misery like this? Why does she have no children? I know she's married, and she must be approaching forty. In another environment I might learn these things, but as I say, that's not the way of this place.

She comes in and swiftly charms the alarm (and me) with a curse. And before I can ask what she thinks about the meaning of suffering, she's off to eliminate another instance of it.

Nietzsche was last week and is still much on my mind. Miroslav said that if he didn't believe in Jesus he would be a Nietzschean. I believe in Jesus and may be a Nietzschean. Not the whole overwrought overman stuff, and not the conflation of pity and weakness. But I feel in my bones (literally, alas) the truth of Nietzsche's insistence upon confronting reality *as it is*, the iron law of cause and effect that in some instances, as even the staunchest person of faith must admit, God either cannot or will not enter or counter. Nietzsche believed that one could fit oneself to, and in essence conquer, necessity by saying, "Thus I willed it," as if the only thing not subject to iron necessity were the will of the one who recognized it. This seems a step too far. But the burn of being I feel in my bones, which makes life seem so joyful, and the burn of unbeing that rages right alongside, which makes that joy so tragic, seem, ultimately, one thing. As does the need to align my will with it.

Perhaps the question, with regard to suffering and what it will mean in your life, comes down to this: What will be the object of your faith, and what will your act of faith look like? Nietzsche placed great faith both in existence and in himself. For forty-four years and thirteen books this worked well enough (though the loneliness of his soul is obvious). Then, as legend goes, one morning he saw a horse being beaten and all his Übermensch armor disintegrated into madness. He became the thing he'd warned against: pitying, and thus pitiful. There's no obvious allegory here. Nietzsche changed modern thought because of the way his mind was made. He went mad for the same reason. Being and unbeing shared the same vital, fatal fuse. His life might have been different had he been more focused on fully inhabiting his first faith (life) rather than shoring up his second one (self), but his death, which lasted eleven long years, was a matter of molecules clicking into place like an elegant proof.

It's that first faith that remains potent, a prod and tonic for the tendency to see human existence and existence itself as at war with each other. In Albert Camus's *The Plague*, the main character, Dr. Rieux, tries to explain why he continues battling the disease that has destroyed his city when his efforts have made no difference. He is, he admits, simply "fighting against creation as he found it." Rieux's struggle is both heroic and quixotic—heroic *because* quixotic, I think Camus would say—but it leaves him lonely and somewhat dead at the heart. Rieux is beyond Christianity but still breathing its metaphysical fumes (his use of the word "creation" is a tell), one of the most persistent of which is the idea that we are fundamentally at odds with the world we inhabit. In this he differs from Nietzsche. What they share (along with Camus himself) is the ancient intuition that suffering and soul are mysterious cognates.

The man in the chair next to me is in distress. I noticed this when he hobbled in grimacing an hour ago, but it's now worse. There are no secrets in a cancer chair, except the one secret that's not so much a secret as a silence that everyone has agreed not to name. He is naming it. He doesn't want to die. He also doesn't want another cycle of bendamustine, and he doesn't want to be admitted into the hospital to get the transfusion that he obviously needs, and he doesn't want one more goddamn appointment with an ENT to see if something can be done about his mouth sores. It's an impasse, but, like all impasses in this place, only momentary: one of those alternatives, and probably all of them, will occur. The man in the chair next to me knows this, I can tell, just as he knows that to suggest any connection between suffering and the soul can be an obscenity to someone in the midst of it. And not simply an obscenity, but a lie.

This is where Job comes in. Do you remember the story? Here's Wisława Szymborska's helpful "Summary" (translated by Sharon Olds and Grazyna Drabik):

Job, tested severely in body and property, curses human fate. It is grand poetry. Friends arrive. Tearing their robes, they examine Job's guilt before the Lord. Job cries that he has been a just man. Job does not want to talk with them. Job wants to talk with the Lord. The Lord appears riding on a gale. In front of this man torn open to the bone, the Lord praises His works: heaven, seas, earth and animals. And especially Behemoth, and in particular Leviathan, beasts which fill one with pride. It is grand poetry. Job listens—the Lord does not speak to the subject, because the Lord does not want to speak to the subject. Promptly then, Job humbles himself before the Lord. Now things happen quickly. Job recovers his donkeys and camels, his mules and sheep, doubled in number. His skin grows back on his bared skull. And Job accepts it. Job is reconciled. Job does not want to spoil the masterpiece.

The irony is pretty typical of (secular) modern responses to Job. How else to reckon with this disturbing tale in which God and Satan* make a wager over one man's life as if they were mob bosses betting on dogs. Job doesn't love you for who you are, Satan says, but for what you've given him; take away his blessings and he'll curse you. God, whose omniscience apparently ends at the edge of Job's brain, disagrees. Into oblivion goes everything and everyone Job loves. Job is steadfast. Up come the boils all over his body. This all happens in a preface, in prose as practical as a drug pamphlet. Then comes the scream.

The Book of Job is usually read as a theodicy, or at least in light of that inquiry. If God is both all-powerful and all-loving, as scripture tells us, whence the bald boy? Job never stops insisting on his own innocence. His first speech is a piece of pure fury cursing the fact that he was ever born, demanding that his existence be not only erased from the earth but expunged from the mind of God. I think Satan actually wins the bet in the Book of Job. I don't think it's possible to love God without loving creation, and I don't think it's possible to love creation without loving one's own created being. Thus a curse of one's own being is a curse of God's as well. There's no "explanation" of suffering in the Book of Job. I'm not even sure that suffering is its real subject, which I think is mostly focused on how—and indeed whether—a human being can relate to God at all. Job's deepest question is not *Why is this happening to me?* No, his deepest question, even in the worst of his curses, is *Where are you, Lord?*

It takes a while, but eventually God does respond. With a blast of beauty.

---

* Actually "a satan," suggesting he's simply one of many.

Hath the rain a father? or who hath begotten the drops of
dew?

Out of whose womb came the ice? and the hoary frost of
heaven, who hath gendered it?

The waters are hid as with a stone, and the face of the deep is
frozen.

Canst thou bind the sweet influences of Pleiades, or loose the
bands of Orion?

Canst thou bring forth Mazzaroth in his season? or canst thou
guide Arcturus with his sons?

Knowest thou the ordinances of heaven? canst thou set the
dominion thereof in the earth?

Canst thou lift up thy voice to the clouds, that abundance of
waters may cover thee?

Canst thou send lightnings, that they may go and say unto
thee, Here we are?

Who hath put wisdom in the inward parts? or who hath given
understanding to the heart?

Job 38:28–36

These are real questions, in the way the Grand Canyon is a
real question, or *King Lear*. The only medium for an answer is a
life. I can't remember the last time I've been so exhilarated and
appalled by a work of art. I have right here on my cancer chair an
essay that praises Job as "a work of profound theology adorned with
poetry," which is so spectacularly wrong that I've not yet been able
to read the rest of the man's argument. As if the poetry were beside
the point. The poetry is the point. When Job needs to scream his
being to God, it's poetry he turns to. When God finally answers
out of the whirlwind, his voice is verse so overwhelming that Job is

said to "see" it. The speech is a reprimand, yes, but God also allows that Job has "spoken right." It's not obvious what God is referring to here. Job has said a lot of things. But the one thing that he has truly hammered home is that cry of dereliction, destruction, and profane (yet not faithless) rage. Whether Job has torn a rift in the relation of man and God, or simply pointed out one that was really always there, it now can never be altogether repaired or ignored. "Nowhere else in the Bible," writes Carol Newsom, "is such an unrestrained demolition of the traditional image of God carried out as in Job's speeches, words that once let loose have continued to resonate for millennia." The demolition, though, is also a resurrection. God's being, which extends from the center of the atom to the burning edge of the universe and beyond beyond, is what Job must accept. But Job's being, and the rage that now ramifies through the centuries ("I will wreak that hate upon him . . ."), is part of that creation, and thus a part of what God must accept. Jack Miles points out that in the Hebrew Bible this speech of God's is the last word God utters. Through the dreams of Daniel and the joys of Esther, the lamentations of Lamentations and the mighty prayers of Nehemiah, through Chronicles, Ecclesiastes, the Song of Songs: no new word. God hasn't silenced Job. Job has silenced God.

I stare out the window at East Rock. It has begun to snow. To speak of artistic greatness and suffering in the same breath is another potential obscenity. That's what Szymborska is saying—in a work of art, mind you. And yet no real artist ever made a thing that some deep wound didn't first demand. East Rock was formed two-hundred million years ago when Yale was swamp and a thousand-pound piece of fury called the *Dilophosaurus* waded down Chapel Street. It's made of diabase traprock, which contains iron that causes the cliffs to look lumpen and rusty in the wrong light, precise and resplendent in the right one. This is the wrong one. Many buildings in New Haven are made of traprock, including some of the marvelous old churches that grow older and emptier every year as God blinks out brain by brain like the 150 species of flora and fauna that go extinct every day as ecosystems implode. Much of that first rock came from a quarry owned by Eli Whitney, who went to Yale and invented the cotton gin, an ambiguous accomplishment both for himself and for humanity. The design of the cotton gin was poorly patented, easily replicable, and spread rapidly throughout the South with little remuneration for Whitney. Slavery, in 1793, was on the wane because of a decrease in the profitability of tobacco farming, but suddenly cotton production was accelerated beyond any capacity to keep up unless there were—in what far-seeing and no doubt God-fearing brain did this inspiration first occur?—more slaves. Many, many more slaves.

I know all this because of Connecticut-in-a-Box, a monthslong research project assigned to local third graders. This is also the source of my knowledge of sperm whales (the state animal) and the *Dilophosaurus* (state dinosaur). I've dug a bit deeper than my daughters, though. I know, for example, that Eli Whitney died of cancer just one mile (as the pterodactyl flies) from the edge of my cancer chair. He was fifty-nine years old and had married for the first time just eight years earlier. His bride was Henrietta Edwards, the granddaughter of Jonathan Edwards, who is famous for viewing suffering as appropriate and necessary punishment for "Sinners in the Hands of an Angry God." But Edwards had a mystical side and not only believed that Jesus could enter and ease our greatest griefs but actually experienced moments of such ecstatic transport that he wanted only "to lie in the dust, and to be full of Christ alone."

Twaddle, Whitney would have called this, if he could have even been roused to that. Whitney was indifferent to religion. He was also indifferent to poetry, slavery, romance (Mrs. Whitney was as vetted and pedigreed as a prize filly), and pretty much anything that didn't have a wood screw or interlocking teeth, but in that realm he was supremely gifted. One of Whitney's biographers argues convincingly that Whitney's life and mind anticipate us, who as a culture value self-reliance over piety, technology over poetry, know-how over knowledge. He never wavered. Near the end of his life, suffering intensely, he ignored the entreaties of friends anxious about the state of his soul and instead spent all his time designing and constructing a device that might ease the pain, which he compared to "the rack of the Inquisition." It's hard to describe extreme pain, and the pain of cancer has an otherworldly intimacy that makes it almost impervious to words. It feels like existence itself is eating you.

Anyway, the world's first flexible catheter—for that's what it probably was, the device that Whitney fashioned out of misery, metal, and whatever other materials his family would not deign to name. ("Indelicate," they said.) It brought him immense relief and might very well have brought him abundant money had he not been preoccupied with dying, and had his family not been too embarrassed to patent the device. By that point it didn't matter: they'd all become wealthy manufacturing guns. Better to cause, rather than ease, pain. A true Last Man, old Eli.

Whitney left behind three young children. The second of these, Elizabeth Fay, was named after Whitney's mother, who took to bed when Eli was six and stayed there until her death seven years later. She was worn out "by bearing four children within five years and by the numberless tasks of the eighteenth-century farm household." Hard not to hear a cry inside that silence. Hard not to think, when Whitney called his daughter's name in his last years, that he wasn't sounding a sorrow that everything else in his life had been designed to eradicate. Little Elizabeth survived her father for twenty-nine years and died at thirty-four. Of her life I know only (from a church record) that she was "admitted to the church on profession, in her sick room." Perhaps she inherited her father's religious indifference but panicked at the end. Or perhaps faith, like a gene that has skipped a generation, lay latent within her, and it took pain to activate it. Or perhaps every single day of her short life was a war of meaning and meaninglessness for her, and the way the coin landed at the last was pure chance.

One human face is as opaque as the point where time began. And we live in an age of hordes, numberless floods. In 2005, newly diagnosed but not yet ill, I went to Moscow for a literary festival. It was a mistake. I couldn't focus on a sentence, much less a city. On the last day, numbly wandering the streets, I found myself standing in front of a memorial for the Russians who lost their lives in World War II. All twenty-six million of them. I felt sickened, not from moral revulsion but from vertigo—the steep meaninglessness of that number. One of those twenty-six million was the newborn daughter of a young female radio operator who went with her unit into a swamp to hide from approaching Germans. The baby began to cry from hunger, but the woman, half-starved herself, could produce no milk. The Germans and their dogs came closer and closer. They were not known for their pity. Can you see her? Thirtyish, up to her waist in water, her breasts exposed, trying to muffle the child's cries. *Where are you, Lord?*

GOD'S JUSTICE

In the beginning there were days set aside for various tasks.
On the day He was to create justice
God got involved in making a dragonfly

and lost track of time.
It was about two inches long
with turquoise dots all down its back like Lauren Bacall.

God watched it bend its tiny wire elbows
as it set about cleaning the transparent case of its head.
The eye globes mounted on the case

rotated this way and that
as it polished every angle.
Inside the case

which was glassy black like the windows of a downtown bank
God could see the machinery humming
and He watched the hum

travel all the way down turquoise dots to the end of the tail
and breathe off as light.
Its black wings vibrated in and out.

This poem by Anne Carson is basically the Book of Job in eigh-
teen lines. On the day that "make justice" appears in God's plan-
ner, he starts doodling in the margin and, God's being being what
it is, raptures into time the world's first dragonfly. God, like any art-
ist, prefers things to themes, prizes the individual instance over the
abstract category. Thus the sun went down on the day of justice,
and God, if human history is any indication, never got back to the
task. Twenty-six million Russians in one war, sixty million Africans
dead in the slave trade, every single face as replete and opaque as
some holy book in a language there's no one left alive to read.

Yet note how that insect is described. The universe is 13.8 billion years old. The first insects emerged about 412 million years ago, but the biblical language puts that dragonfly—along with Adam and Eve—in the primordial soup. Especially Eve. The comparison with Lauren Bacall suggests a connection between kinds of beauty, or suggests, rather, that there is always and only one beauty, which is coextensive with the life of God. Bacall, along with the bank windows, brings us all the way into the present, too. If all beauty is contained in one instance of it, all time is contained in this (any?) moment of creation. Humans are not separate or different from nature—there is in fact no word for "nature" in the Bible—our existence not fundamentally different from existence itself. And what is the "nature" of that existence? God sees the *machinery* humming. "The beauty of the world," says Simone Weil, "gives us an intimation of its claim to a place in our heart. In the beauty of the world brute necessity becomes an object of love."

Of course this means nothing when confronted with the slaughterhouse of history. Of course it means nothing when some pain is tearing your heart in two. Of course, of course, of course. One considers the meaning of suffering only when one is not actually suffering—again, like joy. Frustrated with the line between life and literature, Svetlana Alexievich sought a form that fused the two. From interviews, letters, bits of history that History did not want, she compiled *The Unwomanly Face of War: An Oral History of Women in World War II*, which I picked idly off a library cart while my daughters scoured the shelves for graphic novels. That's where I learned about the radio operator drowning her own infant. And the "sniper girls" who, as they became increasingly expert at death, found themselves falling in love. And the woman who among all the atrocities thought nothing so awful as the neighing of wounded horses ("They're not guilty of anything, they don't answer for human deeds"). One has the fair hair and skin of her mother, the other the olive skin and dark eyes of mine. One absorbs the poems I recite, occasionally saying one back to me suddenly without ever having seen it written down. The other, alone among the family, can sing, and sometimes in the midst of some banal activity will thoughtlessly tear the top of the house off with a high C. Beauty is not *compensatory* for the lack of justice in this life. That's not what that Anne Carson poem is saying. It's saying that God's justice and the beauty of the world are—to the eye that will rise to the sight, or to the eye that grace gives access—one thing. One day God loses himself designing a dragonfly. The next day, who knows, he might have become equally involved in the design of a cancer cell.

Miroslav says some thinkers believe all existence is intertwined and some believe there is a crack that runs through creation. For the first group the task of existence is to match one's mind to that original unity. For the latter the task is one of repair, resistance, and/or rescue.

Predictably, I find myself in both camps. I think all creation is unified; the expression of this feeling is called faith. And I think a crack runs through all creation; that crack is called consciousness. So many ways to say this. I know in my bones there is no escape from necessity, and know in my bones that God's love reaches into and redeems every atom that I am. I believe the right response to reality is to bow down, and I believe the right response to reality is to scream. Life is tragic and faith is comic. Life is necessity and love is grace. (Reality's conjunction is always *and*.) I have never felt quite at home in this world, and never wanted a home altogether beyond it.

Does that make sense? Of course it doesn't. Perhaps it's not all that different from Camus's sense of the absurd (and I do treasure the example of Camus) though it doesn't leave one (I hope), like

Dr. Rieux, alone and dead at heart. But we *are* alone, someone might argue (Nietzsche: "Our personal and profoundest suffering is incomprehensible and inaccessible to almost everyone"), and eventually every heart does go dead (Weil: "Every second which passes brings some being in the world nearer to something he cannot bear"). The first assertion seems debatable, and not simply for the religious. We are not as atomized as that. Atoms are not as atomized as that. Even trees, scientists have learned, communicate sympathetically through the soil and air. Surely such communions are ours as well. But the second assertion, Weil's *drip drip* of instants, seems incontrovertible. The Russian radio operator slowly lowering her infant under the water, Nietzsche crumbling into insanity at the sight of a suffering animal, Eli Whitney with his burning bowels, the young mother and the old child outside the cancer garden at 9:52 a.m., February 11, 2019.

God wears himself out through the infinite thickness of time and space in order to reach the soul and to captivate it. If it allows a pure and utter consent (though brief as a lightning flash) to be torn from it, then God conquers that soul. And when it has become entirely his he abandons it. He leaves it completely alone and it has in its turn, but gropingly, to cross the infinite thickness of time and space in search of him whom it loves. It is thus that the soul, starting from the opposite end, makes the same journey that God made towards it. And that is the cross.

Simone Weil, *Gravity and Grace*

The cross. Of course I end up here. These are, after all, divinity students I'm preparing to teach, though these days many of them seem to me half-atheist. Weil herself was half-atheist. Camus seems to me half-Christian. Anne Carson describes herself as an atheist but can't stop writing about God and goes to Catholic mass because "a kind of thinking takes place there that doesn't take place anywhere else." Thinking or feeling? Weil believed a mystical experience was the only possible knowledge of God. She herself had such an experience and spent the rest of her life crossing "the infinite thickness of time and space" to find its source. Job's vision of God is a mystical experience that doesn't make sense of suffering but renders the question—not irrelevant, exactly, but relevant only to one whose entire orientation to reality has been tried and transformed. "Wilt thou hunt the prey for the lion," asks God (not without irony) and "Who provideth for the raven his food?" By which God means to say that this marvel of creation, this infinite flood of love, is steeped in gore; that "the whole creation groaneth and travaileth in pain together" (Saint Paul); that "beauty is but the beginning of terror we're still just able to bear" (Rilke); that "I think of suffering as the highest form of information, having a direct connection with mystery" (Alexievich); that "the soul has to go on loving in the emptiness, or at least go on wanting to love" (Weil); that "there's no way not to suffer. But you try all kinds of ways to keep from drowning in it, to keep on top of it, and to make it seem—well, like *you*" (Baldwin); that "to be afraid of this death he was staring at with animal terror meant to be afraid of life" (Camus) and "life was dearer to me than all my wisdom ever was" (Nietzsche).

I'm done. Jessica pulls the IV out as if my arm were water. On a cooking show someone's stuffing something. It's not snowing anymore. It's not even winter anymore. Suffering is over. Third grade is over. Connecticut is boxed and basemented and the girls have moved on to Mount Everest and the Mariana Trench in the lavishly illustrated almanac I bought them. They have scoured the sands of the Afar Triangle to find *Australopithecus* AL 288–1, Lucy, Dinknesh ("the wondrous one"), our only Eve. Soon—this very evening, perhaps—we will all go to Galapagos, home of the vampire finch, an affable little bird that nests on the ground, has elaborate and entirely different songs for different islands, and feeds on blood.

50

NO OMEN BUT AWE

I thought it would all resolve
one day in diamond time.
Life like a gem to lift to the squint
as through a jeweler's loupe.

I thought every facet and flaw
neither facet nor flaw in some final shine;
chance and choice uncanny cognates;
form, fate.

Now I am here.
No diamond, no time, no omen but awe
that a whirlwind could in not cohering cohere.
Loss is my gift, bewilderment my bow.

ZERO

You thought it was over? So did I.

  We say we are "in" despair but do we ever say we are "out" of it? Beyond? Above? Every preposition is slightly awry. "What falls away is always," writes Theodore Roethke. "And is near."

  (On the other hand:

Job Davies, eighty-five
Winters old, and still alive
After the slow poison
And treachery of the seasons.

Miserable? Kick my arse!
It needs more than the rain's hearse,
Wind-drawn to pull me off
The great perch of my laugh.

R. S. Thomas, "Lore")

  Late in the writing of this book someone asked me which Dickinson poem "zero at the bone" came from and I couldn't even remember. I pulled out my phone and found, to my delight and disquiet, the "narrow fellow in the grass," the ur-serpent I conjure in entry number fourteen, sliding chillingly through Dickinson's #1096. The mind makes connections the mind knows nothing of.

  In the Zohar, as Fanny Howe noted a hundred pages ago (entry thirty-six), zero is another name for God. That shape without beginning or end, that emptiness that is All.

("Is there a God beside me," Yahweh thunders through the mouth of Isaiah. "Yea, there is no God." An arresting way to put it. Hard not to hear a hyphen implied, no-God as God's identical twin.)*

The Zohar—not that I have read it, not really, just piecemeal gleanings here and there, like everything else in case you haven't noticed by this point; you try living with this Ninja blender for a brain—also says that real tears are a prayer beyond words and famously uses the phrase "spark of darkness" as a metaphor for the enabling/disabling experience of the living God.

Can I claim this? Probably any truly freed soul wouldn't be tempted by the word "claim."

Humans came to the concept of zero relatively late, though it seems certain that dolphins, primates, parrots, and who knows what else had been making unwritten use of it for eons. Even bees, scientists have learned, can distinguish between blank cards and cards with multiple dots, which suggests that they, too, have some notion of nought. Ponder that: nullity and infinity alive in the brain of a bee.†

(I've never written a book in which the last sentence was actually written last. It seems that's where I'm headed, though I've spent weeks at this very spot, stuck in some circle that will not quite close.)

(There's no such thing as a perfect circle. Outside of mathematics, that is, in the world. Or rather, there's no way for us and the world to reach a stasis that would make such measurement

---

* "It is the hallmark of any deep truth that its negation is also a deep truth" (Niels Bohr).

† In fact, as I recall, bees can only go up to six or so, but I mean *unconsciously* alive, or perhaps better, *instinctively* alive, which is also the only way infinity is "alive" for/in us.

possible. Make of that what you will. I'm talking to myself: *Make of that what you will.*)

The brain of a bee. The mind of a hive.

That's how we usually think of it, the hive functioning as one organism. In fact, bees belong in a category known as "super-organisms" wherein individuals are analogous to individual neurons in the brain. One bee might deviate, but the psychophysical laws that govern the whole still obtain. And the deviant suffers.

Judges, chapter fourteen. Young Samson is on his way to Timnah to court his first Philistine (Delilah was the second) when out of nowhere, like the embodiment of Nowhere, a lion charges him. Enraged, inspired ("The Spirit of the Lord came mightily upon him"), Samson tears the creature apart with his bare hands.

Time passes. Samson, betrothed now, on his way home from wars and whatnot, saunters by the same spot and discovers that bees have nested in the carcass. Amazing, he thinks, as he scoops up tons of honey to share with (and to impress) friends and family.

Dire consequences—and centuries of commentary—ensue. Samson was breaking religious law, first in marrying a Philistine woman, secondly in touching something dead, never mind actually looting the corpse for food. He has, like an errant neuron, sought to be better than the Judaic brain of which he was mere part. He has misunderstood, and therefore misused, the gift of God. He has tangled up evil and good, grace and fate, inspiration and vanity. Doom glows in the distance like a dawn.

Me, I can't get past that cat and those bees, the lethal sweetness, the sustenance at the heart of harm. The commentators are all wrong. Samson's mistake was thinking he could kill the leopard—lion, I mean—once and for all. There never was a lion. Lion is all there ever was. Zero at the bone.

ACKNOWLEDGMENTS

I'm grateful to the editors of the following magazines and anthologies, in which some of these pieces first appeared: *America, The American Scholar, Commonweal, Harper's Magazine, Image, Jewish Currents, The Kenyon Review, The New Yorker, The New York Times Magazine, Plough, PN Review, Poetry, Revel, Sewanee Review, Times Literary Supplement, Tin House,* and *Together in a Sudden Strangeness: America's Poets Respond to the Pandemic.*

I would also like to thank Alexandra Green, who has been my research assistant for the past three years, and whose keen eye and ear I have come to rely on.

INDEX